I0413285

CYBER THREATS FROM CHINA, RUSSIA, AND IRAN: PROTECTING AMERICAN CRITICAL INFRA-STRUCTURE

HEARING

BEFORE THE

SUBCOMMITTEE ON CYBERSECURITY, INFRASTRUCTURE PROTECTION, AND SECURITY TECHNOLOGIES

OF THE

COMMITTEE ON HOMELAND SECURITY HOUSE OF REPRESENTATIVES

ONE HUNDRED THIRTEENTH CONGRESS

FIRST SESSION

MARCH 20, 2013

Serial No. 113–9

Printed for the use of the Committee on Homeland Security

Available via the World Wide Web: http://www.gpo.gov/fdsys/

U.S. GOVERNMENT PRINTING OFFICE

82–583 PDF   WASHINGTON : 2013

For sale by the Superintendent of Documents, U.S. Government Printing Office
Internet: bookstore.gpo.gov   Phone: toll free (866) 512–1800; DC area (202) 512–1800
Fax: (202) 512–2250   Mail: Stop SSOP, Washington, DC 20402–0001

(II)

CONTENTS

CYBER THREATS FROM CHINA, RUSSIA, AND IRAN: PROTECTING AMERICAN CRITICAL INFRASTRUCTURE

Wednesday, March 20, 2013

U.S. HOUSE OF REPRESENTATIVES,
COMMITTEE ON HOMELAND SECURITY,
SUBCOMMITTEE ON CYBERSECURITY, INFRASTRUCTURE
PROTECTION, AND SECURITY TECHNOLOGIES,
Washington, DC.

The subcommittee met, pursuant to call, at 2:05 p.m., in Room 311, Cannon House Office Building, Hon. Patrick Meehan [Chairman of the subcommittee] presiding.

Present: Representatives Meehan, McCaul, Chaffetz, Rothfus, Perry, Clarke, and Vela.

Mr. MEEHAN. The Committee on Homeland Security's Subcommittee on Cybersecurity, Infrastructure Protection, and Security Technologies will come to order.

The subcommittee is meeting today to examine the cyber threat that is posed by China, Russia, and Iran.

I now recognize myself for an opening statement.

I would like to welcome this distinguished panel, and everyone to today's hearing, which is our first subcommittee hearing of the 113th Congress. This being our first hearing, I would also like to welcome the new Members and extend my appreciation to Chairman McCaul for naming me the Chairman of the crucial subcommittee.

I would also like to recognize, which we don't customarily do, but it is a special opportunity to have 16 students from the Valley Forge Military Academy, which is in my district, so I am privileged on that factor as well, to join us here today.

I had the good privilege to chair the Subcommittee on Counterterrorism and Intelligence in the last Congress, and there are many overlapping issues in the cyber realm. I look forward to engaging on those again in the coming 2 years.

I would also like to begin by taking the opportunity to credit Ranking Member Clarke for her leadership on cybersecurity and the tremendous work she has been doing for some period of time on this issue. I know she has been tied up, but will be joining us very shortly. Representative Clarke has been at this for a while and I look forward to working together in a bipartisan fashion as we move forward on the issue.

I would also like to salute Dan Lungren—take an opportunity to say thank you to him for his previous Chairmanship of this sub-

(1)

committee and the very, very important work he did on this issue before. His substance, knowledge, and exceptional legal acumen is going to missed by our body, and I wish him well and thank him for his service.

I am looking forward to serving with each of the new Members who will join us here on this committee.

Today's hearing is timely and very relevant. We are examining the cyber threat today that is posed by nation-states, namely China, Russia, and Iran. I focus on the nation-state aspect of this threat because it represents a new battlefield in state relationships and one in which we must prepare accordingly.

Since the new year, there have been significant developments in the cyber domain, highlighted by the fact that the U.S. Government has finally begun to name the nation-states most responsible for cyber attacks against the United States. I believe identifying the threat is critical to combating this problem and protecting our critical infrastructure.

Over the last 2 months, the Obama administration has rightly placed cybersecurity at the top of its public agenda. In his State of the Union speech, President Obama specifically cited foreign countries swiping our corporate secrets, attacking our financial institutions, and sabotaging our power grid.

Last week, Tom Donilon, the President's National security adviser, outed China as the place where cyber intrusions are emanating on an unprecedented scale. Also last week, the annual threat assessment by the United States intelligence community delivered to Congress—Director of National Intelligence, James Clapper, named cyber as the top threat to the United States' National security. This represents a major shift in the threat assessment by the United States intelligence community and makes our work on this committee even more important.

Last, President Obama last week discussed cybersecurity during a congratulatory phone call to the new Chinese president. That, coupled with the talks currently taking place or which just have concluded between Secretary Jack Lew and the new leaders in Beijing mean that this is an excellent development for our Nation that this issue has been addressed at the highest levels.

With respect to identifying the threat, this subcommittee has a history of identifying the threat, naming it publicly, often before it manifests itself. In fact, last year, former Representative Lungren and I held a joint subcommittee hearing entitled, "The Iranian Cyber Threat to the Homeland."

We identified Iran as a cyber growing threat. Since that hearing, it has been reported widely that Iran conducted distributed denial-of-service, the DDOS attacks, against multiple American financial institutions.

Both Mr. Cilluffo and Mr. Berman testified at the hearing and accurately predicted Iran's growing intent and capability to conduct a cyber attack against the United States homeland. I credit both of you with foresight on the issue, when many underestimated the Iranian threat in itself, to our Nation, and particularly the Iranian cyber threat. I view today's hearing as a continuation of last year's hearing and look forward to seeing and hearing how you believe it has evolved.

3

With respect to the Iranian cyber threat, I believe clarity is critically important. Iran is the world's largest state sponsor of terrorism and continues to pursue nuclear weapons to, "wipe Israel off the map." In that sense, we must question whether we are dealing with a potentially irrational actor, which makes the Iranian cyber threat even more dangerous.

I believe that any regime willing to detonate a bomb in a Washington, DC, restaurant to assassinate a Saudi ambassador to the United States would truly be willing to conduct a major cyber attack against United States' critical infrastructure. The U.S. Government must make clear to the Iranians our red lines, and if they escalate their attempts to infiltrate our critical infrastructure, we will respond accordingly.

For the Iranians, cyber is just another tool with which to sow terror and to repress its people. In the words of Michael Oren, the Israeli ambassador to the United States, "Iran's main export is murder." It is important we all realize that, especially within the context of cyber.

To ensure we have clarity about the Iranian threat, I would like to enter into the record a February 16 op-ed in *The Wall Street Journal* by Ambassador Oren, which provides great detail on Iran's regime. I have also asked staff to provide a copy of the op-ed to Members at today's hearing and encourage you to read it closely. In my view, we must assess the Iranian cyber threat through Ambassador Oren's perspective, in the context of, and I quote: "murder, bombings, kidnappings, and trade in drugs and guns. The cyber attack capability is increasing and their intent may well be murderous. We must not forget it."

This is the op-ed. I will ask that it be ordered into the record. Without objection, so ordered.

[The information follows:]

ARTICLE SUBMITTED FOR THE RECORD BY CHAIRMAN MEEHAN

IRAN'S GLOBAL BUSINESS IS MURDER INC.

By Michael Oren, February 11, 2013.

> *Bombings in capital cities, kidnappings, trade in drugs and guns—Iranian exports, all. Now Tehran wants nukes.*

A bomb explodes in Burgas, Bulgaria, leaving five Israeli tourists and a local driver dead. Mysteriously marked ammunition kills countless Africans in civil wars. Conspirators plot to blow up a crowded cafe and an embassy in Washington, DC. A popular prime minister is assassinated, and a despised dictator stays in power by massacring his people by the tens of thousands.

Apart from their ruthlessness, these events might appear unrelated. And yet the dots are inextricably linked. The connection is Iran.

In 25 cities across five continents, community centers, consulates, army barracks and houses of worship have been targeted for destruction. Thousands have been killed. The perpetrators are agents of Hezbollah and the Quds Force, sometimes operating separately and occasionally in unison. All take their orders from Tehran.

Hezbollah's relationship with Tehran is "a partnership arrangement with Iran as the senior partner," says America's director of national intelligence, James Clapper. The Lebanon-based terror group provides the foot soldiers necessary for realizing Iran's vision of a global Islamic empire. Hezbollah chief Hassan Nasrallah says his organization was founded to forge "a greater Islamic republic governed by the Master of Time [the Mahdi] and his rightful deputy, the jurisprudent Imam of Iran."

With funding, training, and weapons from Iran, Hezbollah terrorists have killed European peacekeepers, foreign diplomats, and thousands of Lebanese, among them Prime Minister Rafiq Hariri. They have hijacked American, French, and Kuwaiti

4

airliners and kidnapped and executed officials from several countries. They are collaborating in Bashar Assad's slaughter of opposition forces in Syria today.

A deadly suicide attack in Burgas leaving five Israeli tourists and a local driver dead in last July.

Second only to al-Qaeda, Hezbollah has murdered more Americans—at least 266—than any other terrorist group. The United States designated Hezbollah as a terrorist organization in 1997, though the European Union has yet to do so.

Above all, Hezbollah strives to kill Jews. It has fired thousands of rockets at Israeli civilians and tried to assassinate Israeli diplomats in at least six countries. Its early 1990s bombing of a Jewish community center and the Israeli Embassy in Argentina killed 115.

The attack in Burgas occurred last July, and this month the Bulgarian government completed a thorough inquiry into who was behind it: Hezbollah. "The finding is clear and unequivocal," said John Kerry in one of his first pronouncements as U.S. Secretary of State. "We strongly urge other governments around the world—and particularly our partners in Europe—to take immediate action and to crack down on Hezbollah."

Then there is the Quds Force, the elite unit of Iran's Revolutionary Guard Corps, which takes orders directly from Iranian Supreme Leader Ali Khamenei. The U.S. has repeatedly accused the Quds Force of helping insurgents kill American troops in Iraq and Afghanistan, and of supplying weapons to terrorists in Yemen, Sudan, and Syria. In 2007, Quds Force operatives tried to blow up two Israeli jetliners in Kenya and kill Israel's ambassador in Nairobi.

Hezbollah and the Quds Force also traffic in drugs, ammunition, and even cigarettes. Such illicit activities might seem disparate but they, too, are connected to terror and to Tehran.

In 2011, the *New York Times* reported that Hezbollah was working with South American drug lords to smuggle narcotics into Africa, the Middle East, and Europe. The terror group laundered its hundreds of millions of dollars in profits through used-car dealerships in America.

Also in 2011, the FBI exposed a plot in which senior Quds Force operatives conspired with members of Mexico's Los Zetas drug cartel to assassinate Saudi Arabia's ambassador to Washington by bombing the restaurant where he dined. The Israeli Embassy in Washington was also targeted. The middleman between the terrorists and the drug dealers was an Iranian-American used-car salesman.

And still the dots proliferate. U.S. authorities have implicated Hezbollah in the sale of contraband cigarettes in North Carolina, and Iran has manufactured and sold millions of rounds of ammunition to warring armies in Africa. So while skirting Western sanctions, Iran funds terror world-wide.

But Iran's rulers are counting on the West's inability to see the larger pattern. Certainly the European Union would take a crucial step forward by designating Hezbollah a terrorist organization, but terror is only one pixel.

Tehran is enriching uranium and rushing to achieve military nuclear capabilities. If it succeeds, the ayatollahs' vision of an Islamic empire could crystallize.

Iran and its proxies have already dotted the world with murderous acts. They need only nuclear weapons to complete the horrific picture.

Mr. Oren is Israel's ambassador to the United States.

Mr. MEEHAN. We are joined today by the chief security officer of Mandiant Corporation, who is here to testify on the cyber threat posed by China. While I have already mentioned the administration's naming of the Chinese threat, a great deal of credit goes to Mandiant for its long-term work identifying the specific Chinese military unit responsible for looting our intellectual property and technological innovations and for publicly naming its actual geographic location. That threat is a service—that report is a service to all policymakers trying to combat the Chinese cyber threat.

I also look forward to hearing from today's witnesses with respect to the threat from Russia. Russia is often overlooked in the cyber-threat realm, but they have capability and have illustrated the intent to use it in Estonia and Georgia.

While we fear the theft of classified information, intellectual property, and source codes, as well as grave, crushing attacks on our critical infrastructure from nations who aim to harm us, the threat of monetary and identity theft of our citizens remains a top concern. As our traditional adversary in the game of espionage, I view cyber space as a new, modern Cold War battlefield between the United States and Russia, and we must prepare to respond appropriately.

Let me close my comments by focusing on today's hearing. The point that I believe it is worth pointing out that North Korea has been the source of increased rhetoric pertaining to nuclear weapons, and the Obama administration has responded by announcing the addition of missile interceptors in Alaska over the last few years. North Korea's cyber capability should not be underestimated and its intent is difficult to assess.

I note for the record, as recently as today, the incidents which are being attributed to North Korea by many with respect to the denial of services on banking and communications entities in South Korea, another escalation in the tension between those two, but seen by many—and I may be interested in the testimony of this distinguished panel—to be in response to actions by the United Nations and other civilized countries to rein in the Iranian—I mean the North Korean nuclear capability.

So once again we are seeing this connection of cyber activity in relation to efforts by the civilized world to address both Iran and North Korea.

As Chairman McCaul indicated in last week's full committee hearing, the committee plans to pass cybersecurity legislation in the coming weeks and months. We have been meeting with stakeholder groups affected by this issue, and we encourage continued dialogue.

The vast majority of critical infrastructure is owned by the private sector, so there must be a true partnership between Government and industry to ensure we are protected. I look forward to a continuing conversation on these issues.

Now, let me take a moment to recognize the Ranking Member, and I appreciate that she had been hustling over after being tied up with some other responsibilities. But it is a great privilege to be able to share this responsibility on this committee with my good friend, the gentlelady from New York. As I had identified at the outset, we have been working already together with our staffs.

But I respectfully—I respect greatly the great body of work which the Ranking Member has already put into this issue from her previous service. I look forward in working together with her as this committee moves forward on this very, very important work.

So let me turn it over to the Ranking Member. Thank you.

[The statement of Chairman Meehan follows:]

STATEMENT OF CHAIRMAN PATRICK MEEHAN

MARCH 20, 2013

I'd like to welcome everyone to today's hearing, which is our first subcommittee hearing of the 113th Congress. This being our first hearing, I'm going to take care of a few housekeeping items right off the bat.

As some of you know, I chaired the Subcommittee on Counterterrorism and Intelligence last Congress. There are many overlapping issues in the cyber realm and I look forward to engaging in them over the next 2 years.

I'd like to begin by taking the opportunity to credit Ranking Member Clarke for her leadership on cybersecurity. You have been at this for a while and I look forward to working together in a bipartisan manner moving forward.

Second, I'd also like to take the opportunity to salute the former Chairman of this subcommittee, Rep. Dan Lungren from California. Rep. Lungren served in Congress during the 1980s and after a stint at Attorney General of California in 1990s, felt compelled to serve again after September 11. He was elected to the House again in 2004 and was involved in virtually every post-9/11 Government policy response. His substance, knowledge, and exceptional legal acumen will be missed in this body. I wish him well and thank him for his service.

Finally, I'd like to welcome the new Members to the subcommittee. In my experience, this committee has operated in a bipartisan manner and I expect that to continue in the 113th Congress. I look forward to working with all of you.

Today's hearing is timely and relevant. We are examining the cyber threat posed by nation states: China, Russia, and Iran. I focus on the "nation-state" aspect of this threat because it represents a new battlefield in state relations and we must prepare accordingly.

Since the New Year, there have been significant developments in the cyber domain, highlighted by the fact the U.S. Government has finally begun to name the nation-states most responsible for cyber attacks against the United States. I believe identifying the threat is critical to combatting this problem and protecting our critical infrastructure.

Over the last 2 months, the Obama administration has rightly placed cybersecurity at the top of the public agenda. In his State of the Union speech, President Obama specifically cited "foreign countries" swiping our corporate secrets, attacking our financial institutions, and sabotaging our power grid.

While he didn't name any specific countries, last week, Tom Donilon, the President's National Security Advisor, outed China as the place where cyber intrusions are emanating on "an unprecedented scale."

Also last week, in the Annual Threat Assessment by the U.S. intelligence community delivered to Congress last week, the Director of National Intelligence (DNI), James Clapper, named cyber as the top threat to U.S. National security. This represents a major shift in the threat assessment by the U.S. intelligence community and makes our work on this committee even more important.

Last, *The New York Times* reported last week the President Obama discussed cybersecurity during a congratulatory phone call with the new Chinese President. The fact this issue is being addressed at the head-of-state level is an excellent development. I credit the Obama administration for naming the threat and pushing for action.

With respect to identifying the threat, this subcommittee has a history of identifying the threat and naming it publicly, often before it manifests itself. In fact, last year, former Rep. Lungren and I held a joint subcommittee hearing entitled, "The Iranian Cyber Threat to the Homeland" which identified Iran as a growing cyber threat.

Since that hearing, it has been widely reported that Iran conducted distributed denial-of-service (DDoS) attacks against multiple American financial institutions. If true, I'd say that we were all correct in our predictions last July. Both Mr. Cilluffo and Mr. Berman testified at that hearing and aptly predicted Iran's growing intent and capability to conduct a cyber attack against the U.S. homeland. I credit you both for your foresight on this issue when many underestimated the Iranian cyber threat.

I view today's hearing as a continuation of last year's hearing and I look forward to learning how the threat has evolved.

With respect to the Iranian cyber threat, I believe clarity is critically important. Iran is the world's largest state sponsor of terrorism and continues to pursue nuclear weapons to "wipe Israel off the map." In that sense, I believe we are dealing with a potentially irrational actor, which makes the Iranian cyber threat even more dangerous.

Common sense dictates that any regime willing to detonate a bomb at a Washington, DC restaurant to assassinate the Saudi Ambassador to the United States would surely be willing to conduct a major cyber attack against U.S. critical infrastructure. The U.S. Government must make clear to the Iranians our "red lines" and make clear to them that if they escalate any cyber attacks against U.S. critical infrastructure, we will respond appropriately.

For the Iranians, cyber is just another tool through which to sow terror and repress its people. In the words of my good friend Michael Oren, Israeli Ambassador to the United States, Iran's main export is murder. It is important we all realize that, especially within the context of cyber.

To that ensure we have the clarity about the Iranian threat, I would like to enter into the record a February 16 op-ed in *The Wall Street Journal* by Ambassador Oren entitled "Iran's Global Business is Murder, Inc." The op-ed provides great detail on Iran's murderous regime. I have also asked staff to ensure a copy of the op-ed has been provided to Members at today's hearing and encourage you to read it closely.

In my view, we must assess the Iranian cyber threat through Ambassador Oren's perspective: "in the context of murder, bombings, kidnappings, and trade in drugs and guns." Their cyber attack capability is increasing and their intent is murderous. We must not forget it.

Without objection, so ordered.

Members are also lucky to have a representative from Mandiant Corp. here today to testify on the cyber threat posed by China. While I've already mentioned the administration's naming of the Chinese threat, a great deal of credit goes to Mandiant for its long-term work identifying the specific Chinese military unit responsible for looting our intellectual property and technological innovations and publicly naming its actual geographic location. That report is a service to all policymakers trying to combat the Chinese cyber threat.

As the ultimate credit to Mandiant's report on China's cyber threat, I will quote perhaps the premier American intelligence official, former CIA and NSA Director and fellow Pennsylvanian, General Michael Hayden, who simply stated: "It was a wonderful report." General Hayden knows a thing or two about intelligence analysis so I view this as the ultimate validation of Mandiant's work.

With respect to the Russian cyber threat, I look forward to hearing from today's witnesses. Russia is often overlooked in the cyber threat realm, but they have the capability and have illustrated the intent to use it in Estonia and Georgia.

As our top traditional adversary in the game of espionage, I view cyber space as a new, modern Cold War battlefield between the United States and Russia and we must prepare and respond appropriately. While not the focus of today's hearing, I believe it is worth pointing out that North Korea has been the source of increased rhetoric pertaining to nuclear weapons and the Obama administration has responded by announcing the addition of missile interceptors in Alaska over the next few years.

North Korea's cyber capability should not be underestimated and its intent is difficult to assess. It was widely reported North Korea conducted cyber attacks against South Korea and the United States in July 2009. We must keep a watchful eye on this continued threat actor.

As Chairman McCaul indicated at last week's full committee hearing, the committee plans to pass cybersecurity legislation in the coming weeks and months. We have been meeting with stakeholder groups affected by this issue and we encourage continued dialogue. The vast majority of critical infrastructure is owned by the private sector so there must be a true partnership between Government and industry to ensure we are protected.

I look forward to continuing the conversation on these issues.

Ms. CLARKE. I thank you, Mr. Chairman, and I thank you for holding this hearing today.

First, I would like to congratulate you, Chairman Meehan, on your appointment to Chair of our subcommittee. I look forward to working with you to continue this subcommittee's proud history of bipartisan oversight and legislative action.

I think that the topic at hand is an appropriate one for our subcommittee's first hearing at this Congress. I don't have to tell you, Mr. Chairman, that the cyber threats to our critical infrastructure are growing and serious, and cybersecurity is perhaps the most prominent National security issue we face this Congress.

Last week in the intelligence community's annual world-wide threat assessment report to Congress, Director of National Intelligence, James Clapper, named cyber as the leading threat to our National security, ahead of terrorism, transnational crime, and WMD proliferation.

To set the stage for the important actions that our committee must take to enhance our Nation's cybersecurity, it is important that we first examine the evolving nature of the threat we are facing.

Each month seems to bring a new wrinkle in our understanding of the threat to our Government, to our businesses, and to individuals. Malicious cyber actors have destroyed 30,000 computers on an oil company's network in the blink of an eye.

They have bombarded dozens of our banks with denial-of-service attacks on a weekly basis in a concerted campaign dragging on for months. They have infiltrated the manufacturer of smart grid industrial control systems, which are currently installed all across the Nation in our critical infrastructure.

These are just reports that have been made public in the last 9 months. We have long since passed the time when our biggest challenge in cyber space was dealing with the stereotypical teenager in his parent's basement.

A small group of nation-states are taking advantage of the internet's openness to conduct cyber-espionage, not only against traditional Government targets, such as defense and intelligence agencies, but against all variety of economic targets and critical infrastructure.

But though I think we have recognized this for some time, what has been missing is a public discussion of this bad behavior. That is why I think the events of the last few weeks have been a real tipping point in the way our Nation responds to cyber threats.

Foreign actors can no longer be permitted to commit industrial-strength espionage against our Government and businesses without being brought to account. I have been heartened to see that the Obama administration has recently made great strides in this area.

Two weeks ago, National Security Adviser Tom Donilon went on the record about China's aggressive behavior in cyber space, outlining key areas where the United States will require China's engagement moving forward. Then, last week, President Obama himself expanded upon the threat posed by the Chinese and other state actors, and the strong messages that we are beginning to send.

I applaud the administration's willingness to raise this issue to the Presidential level. I hope that it leads to substantive engagement with foreign governments on proper conduct in cyber space.

Finally, I am pleased that we are joined today by this very distinguished panel of witnesses. I look forward to learning more about the cyber threats to our critical infrastructure and further informing the public debate on cybersecurity.

I yield back, Mr. Chairman.

[The statement of Ranking Member Clarke follows:]

STATEMENT OF RANKING MEMBER YVETTE D. CLARKE

MARCH 20, 2013

I think that the topic at hand is an appropriate one for our subcommittee's first hearing this Congress.

I do not have to tell you, Mr. Chairman, that the cyber threats to our critical infrastructure are growing and serious, and cybersecurity is perhaps the most prominent National security issue we will face this Congress.

Last week, in the intelligence community's Annual Worldwide Threat Assessment report to Congress, Director of National Intelligence James Clapper named cyber as the leading threat to our National security, ahead of terrorism, transnational crime, and WMD proliferation.

To set the stage for the important actions that our committee must take to enhance our Nation's cybersecurity, it is important that we first examine the evolving nature of the threat we are facing.

Each month seems to bring a new wrinkle in our understanding of the threat to our Government, to our businesses, and to individuals.

Malicious cyber actors have destroyed 30,000 computers on an oil company's network in the blink of an eye.

They have bombarded dozens of our banks with denial-of-service attacks on a weekly basis in a concerted campaign dragging on for months.

They have infiltrated the manufacturer of smart grid industrial control systems which are currently installed all across the country in our critical infrastructure.

These are just reports that have been made public in the last 9 months.

We have long since passed the time when our biggest challenge in cyber space was dealing with the stereotypical teenager in his parents' basement.

A small group of nation-states are taking advantage of the internet's openness to conduct cyber espionage, not only against traditional Government targets such as defense and intelligence agencies, but against all variety of economic targets and critical infrastructure.

But though I think we have recognized this for some time, what has been missing is a public discussion of this bad behavior.

That's why I think the events of the last few weeks have been a real tipping point in the way our Nation responds to cyber threats.

Foreign actors can no longer be permitted to commit industrial-strength espionage against our Government and businesses without being brought to account, and I have been heartened to see that the Obama administration has recently made great strides in this area.

Two weeks ago, National Security Advisor Tom Donilon went on the record about China's aggressive behavior in cyber space, outlining key areas where the United States will require China's engagement moving forward.

Then, last week, President Obama himself expanded upon the threat posed by the Chinese and other state actors and the strong messages that we are beginning to send.

I applaud the administration's willingness to raise this issue to the Presidential level, and I hope that it leads to substantive engagement with foreign governments on proper conduct in cyber space.

Finally, I am pleased that we are joined today by this distinguished panel of witnesses, and I look forward to learning more about the cyber threats to our critical infrastructure and further informing the public debate on cybersecurity.

Mr. MEEHAN. Well, thank you, Ranking Member Clarke.

One little housekeeping issue here, because one of the realities of our work here in Congress is the most important responsibility, which is to vote, and as you can see, we were just called to vote.

So I am going to use the little window that we have here to try to do some quick introductions of our panel, and then I am going to ask—we are going to try to get through the testimony of two of the first witnesses.

We will then quickly return from votes and, hopefully, gavel it down as quickly as we can after we are finished voting to hear the testimony of the last two, and then we will move into questions from the Members who are able to join us again. So let us—the rest of the committee is reminded, opening statements can be submitted for the record.

[The statement of Ranking Member Thompson follows:]

STATEMENT OF RANKING MEMBER BENNIE G. THOMPSON

MARCH 20, 2013

The list of significant cyber intrusions against our critical infrastructure keeps growing.

Our top Government officials are going on the record about state sponsors of aggressive cyber activities that have been stealing our trade secrets and intellectual property as well as targeting our most sensitive critical infrastructure networks.

National Security Advisor Tom Donilon and Director of National Intelligence James Clapper have spent recent weeks identifying state sponsors of aggressive cyber activities—including China, Iran, and Russia.

Just last week, President Obama raised the issue of cyber attacks with the Chinese president, instantly raising the importance of cybersecurity in the U.S.-China relationship.

But even though we have made great strides in our response to state-sponsored cyber activities, we cannot expect the problem to go away overnight.

It would be prudent to expect the future to bring new, more sophisticated attacks.

Even the best, most secure critical infrastructure in our country is no match for a determined adversary backed by the resources of a government.

That is why it is so important for this committee to pass comprehensive cybersecurity legislation.

We must act to provide a framework which will improve the partnership between the owners and operators of our critical infrastructure and the Government to work together collaboratively to protect our networks.

I look forward to working with you, Chairman Meehan and Ranking Member Clarke, as well as Chairman McCaul, to ensure that this legislative necessity becomes a reality.

But while the threats we face are severe, it is important that we do not overstate them or call for a militarized response.

Not all attacks require a military response. The vast majority of attacks are against individual citizens and the private sector.

We need a measured civilian response that permits these threats to be addressed by DHS and the FBI working together to mitigate and respond to the attacks, investigate the perpetrators, and help prevent future attacks.

Just last week, NSA Director Keith Alexander testified before Congress that cyber attacks on U.S. soil required a civilian-led response.

The evolution or increase in threats is no justification for abandoning the traditional separation of foreign and domestic intelligence and law enforcement authorities.

We cannot allow cyber attacks to provide a reason to jettison the precious and hard-won American values of privacy and civil liberties.

I am convinced that any measure we put forth must embrace privacy and civil liberties as a bedrock principle.

As we move forward with cybersecurity legislation, with those values firmly embedded, we must take the time to fully investigate and understand the scope of the threats we face.

So, I am pleased that we are joined today by this panel of experts, who can speak to the diverse array of cyber threats to our critical infrastructure, and I look forward to their testimony.

Mr. MEEHAN. Let me now identify the distinguished panel of witnesses before us here today on this topic—and no stranger, any of them, to this issue. Mr. Frank Cilluffo directs the Homeland Security Policy Institute at the George Washington University, where he works on a wide variety of homeland security issues, including counterterrorism, counter security, transportation security, and emergency management.

Mr. Cilluffo joined G.W. in April 2003 after leaving the White House, where he was a special assistant to the President for homeland security.

Mr. Richard Bejtlich is the chief information security officer for Mandiant, the security firm that recently released a widely-publicized report on the hacking activities of the Chinese government. Mr. Bejtlich has more than 13 years' experience of enterprise-level intrusion detection and incident response, working with the Federal Government, defense, and private industry.

Mr. Ilan Berman is the vice president of the American Foreign Policy Council, where he specializes in regional security in the Middle East, Central Asia, and Russia. Throughout his career, Mr. Berman has consulted for numerous Government agencies, including the CIA and the Department of Defense. Mr. Berman has also authored several books, and serves as the editor of The Journal of International Security Affairs.

Mr. Martin Libicki is a senior management scientist at RAND Corporation, where he focuses on the impacts of information technology on domestic and National security. His most recent research has focused on assisting the United States Air Force prepare for cyber war, exploiting cell phones in counterinsurgency, developing post-9/11 information technology strategy for the Department of Justice, and assessing the terrorist information awareness program for the Defense Advanced Research Project Agency.

The witnesses' full written statements will appear in the record, so the Chairman now recognizes Mr. Cilluffo for 5 minutes to testify.

STATEMENTS OF FRANK J. CILLUFFO, DIRECTOR, HOMELAND SECURITY POLICY INSTITUTE, CO-DIRECTOR, CYBER CENTER FOR NATIONAL AND ECONOMIC SECURITY, THE GEORGE WASHINGTON UNIVERSITY

Mr. CILLUFFO. Well, thank you, Mr. Chairman.

Chairman Meehan, Ranking Member Clarke, distinguished Members of the committee; I would like to thank you for the opportunity to appear before you today.

Mr. Chairman, I think you deserve the foresight for having been prescient in terms of identifying the Iranians cyber threat the last go-around. So hats off to you.

Quite honestly, I think we need to have continued leadership on these issues as the threat continues to grow in terms of scale, scope, and the consequences are becoming more and more clear. Put simply, both our National security and our Nation's economic security are at risk, and the stakes are exceedingly high.

When prepping for this hearing and thinking about how to convey a whole lot of information in a very short amount of time, I thought perhaps the best way to do so is to provide a frame for how to think about some of these issues.

I did put in my prepared remarks a couple of charts that get to the point where we can start racking and stacking the threats, understanding the different intentions and capabilities of the actors, and to be able to put it into some sort of context.

I also will be very brief, and I know my fellow witnesses here will touch on all the various specific threats. But I would like to applaud the Mandiant report. I think it provided a smoking keyboard. We have all known about the Chinese activity, but in this case it provided both empirical evidence and did so with strong data. We need more of that in the open community.

Very quickly, a couple of contextual thoughts and assumptions before I jump into the charts. It is becoming more and more clear that the future of conflict will include a cyber component. This is military and other forms of conflict. Computer network operations, including exploits and attacks will be and are being integrated into military planning, doctrine, and operations.

Nations that can best marshal and mobilize their cyber power and integrate it into their strategy in war fighting, I would argue, will ensure significant National security advantage in the future. These efforts not only enhance their ability to project power in terms of a battlefield context, but also to stymie the power of others, and that is important to keep in mind when we are looking at some of the threat actors we are discussing today.

Moreover, not all hacks are the same, nor are all hackers the same. The threat spectrum is wide-ranging. It comes in various shapes, sizes, and forms, ranging from nation-states who are integrating computer network attack and exploit into their war fighting capability down to those kids that are still operating out the basements of their parents' homes. So we do have that broad spectrum.

I would underscore that nations themselves have different capabilities and different intentions. In the charts, what I tried to lay out in a very simple axis is a capability and intent axis, both in terms of what the steady-state threat matrix is to the United States and our homeland and also to what sorts of triggering events could cause an escalation.

I spliced out what I call computer network exploit. Think of that as espionage, traditional espionage: Political, military secret-stealing, but also obviously economic espionage, which is the theft of intellectual property and economic secrets, as well as industrial espionage, where companies are stealing secrets to benefit—where countries are stealing to benefit individual companies. You have got to look at it in all those realms.

Then you have got computer network attack, which is where they turn to computer network attack capabilities to be able to cause harm.

So if you were to rack and stack the various countries we are talking about right now, obviously, China and Russia are what you would call APT threats, advanced persistent threats. They are at the very high end in terms of capability.

When you look at the exploit side or the espionage side, they are blinking to the far right, both in terms of intentions and in terms of capabilities. When you look in terms of computer network attack, they are more on the left axis. In other words, they have some modicum of responsibility and recognize that we could retaliate and have some responsibilities to be able to at least harness some of that capability in a smart way.

When you look at Iran, on the other hand, while the good news they are not at the same level of capability as Russia and China, the bad news is for what they lack in capability, they more than make up for in intent. What intent they don't have, they can turn to their proxies or they can simply buy or rent. Botnets are available for a small amount of money, and they can still cause harm.

But the bar to entry, when we talk about cyber, is not very high. That said, those with more sophisticated capabilities, that they, in my eyes, are a much greater concern.

North Korea, they are the wild card. North Korea, I think clearly has intent, and they are turning to computer network attack. Much like Iran, they are not curtailed in terms of some of their responsibilities in this space. So I put them on the very high end in terms of computer network attack and in terms of consequence and likelihood.

As I know my time is running out, one thing to keep in mind that I think needs to be underscored, and this is with respect to

13

Russia and China. If you can exploit, you can attack. In other words, if they have the intent to attack—we know what they are doing in terms of computer network exploitation. It is brazen. It is wholesale. It is significant.

If their intent is to attack, the same techniques they are using to exploit can be flipped, literally. It is as simple as flipping a switch to attack. Here I think we have to take that very seriously, and there are a whole host of triggering events that could cause that escalation, which I am happy to get into during the Q & A.

Bottom line, we are never going to firewall our way out of this problem. We need to improve our defenses, but we also need to invest in our offensive capabilities and get to a point where we can deter our enemies; dissuade, deter, and compel. I will leave it at that.

Thank you, Mr. Chairman.

[The prepared statement of Mr. Cilluffo follows:]

PREPARED STATEMENT OF FRANK J. CILLUFFO

MARCH 20, 2013

Chairman Meehan, Ranking Member Clarke, and distinguished Members of the subcommittee, thank you for this opportunity to testify before you today. The subcommittee has demonstrated real leadership in this issue area with hearings and other work undertaken long before the cyber domain and its challenges were front and center on the National agenda as is now the case. For example, your hearing last April on the Iranian cyber threat to the United States was quite prescient.[1] That challenge, and the broader one under study today, remains crucial to explore, understand, and respond to, because of all that is at stake—namely U.S. National and economic security.

My statement below is designed to help frame how the United States can and should assess and respond to cyber threats, especially those posed by nation-states. A great deal of excellent, deep-dive analysis is already being performed on specific threats, including the work of my fellow witnesses. For example, the recent Mandiant report tracing extensive hacking activity against the United States (and other countries and corporations) back to the doorstep of China's Army, the PLA, was a significant contribution to the discourse, in that it provided both forensic and empirical data, which are in short supply in the open-source literature, yet sorely needed.[2] What is also needed, however, is a broader typology of the cyber threat, structured to help us rack and stack the challenges that we face, and prioritize our efforts to meet them. I will propose such a typology today to assess the relative severity of cyber threats, and also suggest how the United States might re-focus its cyber efforts accordingly.

The cyber threat comes in various shapes, sizes, and forms. The bar to entry is low to launch a relatively rudimentary, but still potentially damaging, cyber attack. The threat spectrum ranges from nation-states plus their proxies, to foreign terrorist organizations, criminal syndicates and information brokers, to hacktivists, to ankle-biters operating out of their parents' home. Each of these categories, in turn, also breaks down into a number of sub-categories. Regarding nation-states, for example, they vary widely in their sophistication, capability, intent, motivation, and so on. Taking a top-line perspective, however, it is nation-states (and their proxies) that the United States should be most concerned about when it comes to threat. This finding is supported by a recent Homeland Security Policy Institute (HSPI) Flash Poll conducted right after the President issued an Executive Order, "Improv-

---

[1] "The Iranian Cyber Threat to the United States", Testimony of Frank J. Cilluffo before the House Subcommittee on Cybersecurity, Infrastructure Protection, and Security Technologies; and the House Subcommittee on Counterterrorism and Intelligence (April 26, 2012). http://www.gwumc.edu/hspi/policy/Iran%20Cyber%20Testimony%204.26.12%20Frank%20Cilluffo.pdf.
[2] Mandiant Report, "APT-1: Exposing one of China's Cyber Espionage Units" (February 2013). http://intelreport.mandiant.com/, and https://www.mandiant.com/blog/mandiant-exposes-apt1-chinas-cyber-espionage-units-releases-3000-indicators/.

ing Critical Infrastructure Cybersecurity",[3] this February. According to our poll, to which over 100 HSPI stakeholders responded: Nearly 70% of respondents indicated that nation-states posed the greatest threat to cybersecurity, by comparison to other categories of actors. The remainder of responses were split between foreign terrorist organizations, "hacktivists", organized crime, and "other".[4]

For too long, though, we have assessed and appreciated the nation-state threat in overly general terms. The volume and nature of activity directed against us, and our allies, should serve as a wake-up call to raise our game. Now is the time to focus on the high-end threat, and to rack and stack our priorities. We simply cannot afford to do otherwise—not in the current economic climate, and not in light of the critical U.S. assets and infrastructure that are still vulnerable and at risk.

Every day, new news of cyber intrusions, exploits, and attacks comes to light. The Nation's most sensitive sectors, from defense to energy to finance, are often the targets. Our adversaries have engaged in brazen activity, from computer network exploitation (CNE) to computer network attack (CNA). Foreign militaries are, increasingly, integrating CNE and CNA capabilities into their warfighting and military planning and doctrine. These efforts may allow our adversaries to enhance their own weapon systems and platforms, as well as stymie those of others. CNE may also support intelligence preparation of the battlefield, to include the mapping of critical infrastructures that could be targeted in a more strategic campaign or attack plan. CNAs may occur simultaneously with other forms of attack (kinetic, insider threats, etc).

Last month, against this background, the President issued an Executive Order intended to improve critical infrastructure cybersecurity.[5] The goal is closer collaboration between Government and the private sector to protect critical networks. The Executive Order is a good start, but it is no substitute for legislation—which can introduce a range of incentives (such as tax provisions, liability protections, and procurement preferences which factor security requirements into Federal acquisitions) plus sticks to accompany those carrots, and thereby raise the bar higher when it comes to critical infrastructure standards and practices.[6]

To refine and reinforce its stance in relation to the threat, the United States must focus upon actors and their particular behaviors, rather than upon technology per se, or upon means and modalities of attack. Doing so means digging deeper into specifics, and factoring those case-by-case (actor- and country-specific) details about our adversaries into a tailored U.S. response that is also designed to dissuade, deter, and compel our adversaries accordingly. Our response must be calibrated to address and thwart (among other things) the adversary's motivation—be it to steal money, intellectual property, or military secrets, etc. U.S. response must also be calibrated to address and thwart the adversary's intent—be it commercial gain, military advantage, criminal activity, etc. To complicate matters, both motivation and intent are multidimensional, and thus may consist of some combination of these factors. Motivation and intent may also change over time, and the various factors that comprise each may shift at a given moment. Nation-states and their proxies may also differ in their motivation and intent.

Parsing our understanding of U.S. adversaries down to (and beyond) this level of granularity will yield insights upon which more effective strategies and tactics may be built and implemented. At first glance, such a task may seem overwhelming, given the number and complexity of the potential variables. The good news is that a robust but general posture should help us deal with the signal-to-noise ratio and suffice to handle 80% of the nefarious activity that comes our way. The other 20% is where we need to keep a closer eye on the ball. I turn now to those harder cases, to offer a snapshot of who they are, what they have done, why they have done it, and what they might do in future.

Naming and shaming is an approach that has been invoked with varying degrees of success across a range of contexts. Until recently, however, only a few of the boldest of U.S. officials (current and former) had walked out on that limb in the context under examination today. Lately, however, the number of U.S. Government and private-sector voices has become more of a chorus. The President's National Security Advisor Thomas Donilon publicly cited and elaborated upon U.S. cybersecurity con-

---

[3] http://www.whitehouse.gov/the-press-office/2013/02/12/executive-order-improving-critical-infrastructure-cybersecurity.

[4] http://www.gwumc.edu/hspi/frontincludes/Cyber%20EO%20Flash%20Poll%20Press-%20Release%202-15-2013.pdf.

[5] http://www.whitehouse.gov/the-press-office/2013/02/12/executive-order-improving-critical-infrastructure-cybersecurity.

[6] Frank J. Cilluffo and Andrew Robinson, "While Congress dithers, cyber threats grow greater" Nextgov.com (July 24, 2012). http://www.nextgov.com/cybersecurity/2012/07/while-congress-dithers-cyber-threats-grow-greater/56968/.

cerns in connection with China, in a speech earlier this month.[7] Before that, and among other developments, the *New York Times* published an account of intrusions against its own networks[8] by Chinese hackers—which in turn seems to have prompted a cascade of similar revelations, including in relation to the *Washington Post* and the *Wall Street Journal*. In this context, as in others, there is power in numbers.

Capabilities do matter, of course. Our most challenging adversaries in the cyber domain are commonly known as Advanced Persistent Threats (APT). China and Russia indisputably fall in this category although the two can and should be characterized and understood somewhat differently (see below). Iran is another difficult case, though a bit different in kind, as it makes up in intent what it may lack in capability—though its capabilities are noteworthy, especially when proxies are factored in. To the list of truly concerning nation-state actors one could and should also add North Korea. A worst-case scenario would combine kinetic and cyber attacks, and the cyber component would serve as a force multiplier to increase the lethality or impact of the physical attack(s).

Though I will focus exclusively on China, Russia, and Iran in the limited space that remains, North Korea is a troubling case as well as an unusual one. Ordinarily, it is organized crime that seeks to penetrate the state. In this case, however, it is the other way around, with the state trying to penetrate organized crime in order to ensure the survival of the regime/dynasty. Like Iran, the DPRK is more likely to turn to CNA to achieve its objectives. In this regard, Iran and North Korea stand in contrast to China and Russia which operate under greater constraints. Precisely because North Korea has fewer constraints, I would underscore that it poses an important "wild card" threat, not only to the United States but also to the region and broader international stability.

Since a picture is often worth a thousand words, I have tried to encapsulate findings and cross-country comparisons in the two charts that follow. The graphics are a rough attempt to rank each of the countries at issue according to capability and intent, as well as in terms of the CNE and CNA threat that they each pose, including in relative terms to one another. For the purposes of the matrices below, CNE is defined as traditional, economic, and industrial espionage, as well as intelligence preparation of the battlefield (IPB). However, IPB is also included in the definition of CNA used here, as it may well be a precursor, such as surveillance and reconnaissance of targets to be attacked. Bear in mind that if one can exploit, one can also attack if the intent exists to do so. Note also that, for present purposes, CNA is defined as activities that alter (disrupt, destroy, etc.) the targeted data/information.

---

[7] "The United States and the Asia-Pacific in 2013", before The Asia Society (March 11, 2013). *http://www.whitehouse.gov/the-press-office/2013/03/11/remarks-tom-donilon-national-security-advisory-president-united-states-a*.

[8] Nicole Perlroth, "Hackers in China Attacked the Times for Last 4 Months", *New York Times* (January 30, 2013). *http://www.nytimes.com/2013/01/31/technology/chinese-hackers-infiltrate-new-york-times-computers.html?pagewanted=all&_r=0*.

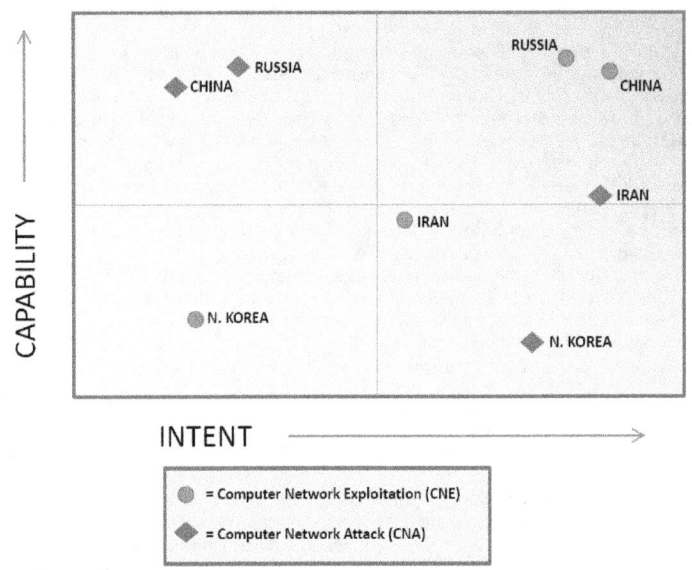

The second chart reflects the shifts in position that may occur if triggering or unforeseen events lead to potential escalation:

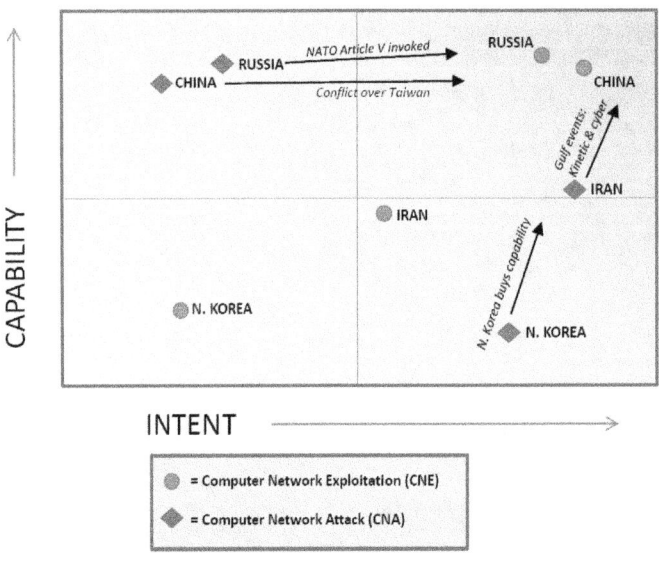

Unless and until we wrap our heads around the challenge posed by each of these cases, and do so in a way that appreciates both the similarities and differences between and among them, our National and economic security (including our critical infrastructure) will remain at risk. Not all actors, nor capabilities, nor intentions, are the same. Tradecraft and its application may also differ widely. So too motivations, which may include blackmail, coercion, fraud, and theft. Heightening our understandings of each of these elements as they apply to key actors is all the more important, as countries continue to integrate CNA/CNE into war-fighting and military planning, and interweave the cyber domain into the activities of their foreign intelligence services, to include intelligence derived from human sources (HUMINT).

China

China possesses sophisticated cyber capabilities and has demonstrated a striking level of perseverance, evidenced by the sheer number of attacks and acts of espionage that the country commits. Reports of the Office of the U.S. National Counterintelligence Executive have called out China and its cyber espionage, characterizing these activities as rising to the level of strategic threat to the U.S. National interest.[9] The U.S.-China Economic and Security Review Commission notes further: "Computer network operations have become fundamental to the PLA's strategic campaign goals for seizing information dominance early in a military operation".[10] China's aggressive collection efforts appear to be intended to amass data and secrets (military, commercial/proprietary, etc.) that will support and further the country's economic growth, scientific and technological capacities, military power, etc.—all with an eye to securing strategic advantage in relation to (perceived or actual) competitor countries and adversaries.

China denies the various charges leveled against it, and has raised its own hacking allegations, in which the country claims to have been victimized. The latter claim is difficult to accept completely, especially since China appears to take its own cybersecurity efforts seriously. According to Microsoft's security blog, "China had the lowest malware infection rate . . . of any of the 105 locations included in volume 13 of the [Microsoft] Security Intelligence Report", which refers back to 2012.[11] Perhaps China is as focused on self-inoculation as it is on hacking others? And perhaps this posture derives from an attempt to protect precisely the points of vulnerabilities that China saw in others? Consider also the Mandiant report referenced earlier, which identifies Chinese PLA Unit 61398 as the most likely culprit behind the theft of "hundreds of terabytes of data from at least 141 organizations across a diverse set of industries, beginning as early as 2006."

As a domain, cyber space is made for plausible deniability. Attribution remains a challenge, because smoking keyboards can be hard to find; and in the case of China, the PLA may also outsource certain activities and operations to skilled hackers, to distance the PLA from any smoking keyboards.[12] The attribution challenge is just one reason the Mandiant report is significant. Separate and apart from attempts to mask involvement in activity targeting the United States, there may also be powerful reasons for China to restrict itself from acting against the United States in certain ways, at least at a particular moment in time. Director of National Intelligence James Clapper testified last week that China and Russia are "advanced" cyber actors, but that he did not foresee "devastating" cyber attacks by these two actors against the United States in the near future [13]—"outside of a military conflict or crisis that they believe threatens their vital interests."[14] The vital interests ca-

[9] "Foreign Spies Stealing U.S. Economic Secrets in Cyberspace", Report to Congress on Foreign Economic Collection and Industrial Espionage, 2009–2011 (October 2011). *http:// www.ncix.gov/publications/reports/fecie_all/Foreign_Economic_Collection_2011.pdf* [referred to hereafter as NCIX Report]. See also Frank J. Cilluffo, "Chinese Telecom Firms Pose a Threat to U.S. National Security", *U.S. News & World Report* (November 19, 2012). *http:// www.usnews.com/opinion/articles/2012/11/19/chinese-telecom-firms-pose-a-threat-to-us-national-security.*

[10] Patton Adams, George Bakos, and Bryan Krekel, "Occupying the Information High Ground: Chinese Capabilities for Computer Network Operations and Cyber Espionage," Report prepared for the U.S.-China Economic and Security Review Commission by Northrop Grumman Corp. (March 3, 2012). *http://www.uscc.gov/RFP/2012/USCC%20Report_Chinese_Capabilities-forComputer_NetworkOperationsandCyberEspionage.pdf.*

[11] Tim Rains, "The Threat Landscape in China: A Paradox" (March 11, 2013). *http:// blogs.technet.com/b/security/*

[12] Perlroth, *http://www.nytimes.com/2013/01/31/technology/chinese-hackers-infiltrate-new-york-times-computers.html?pagewanted=all&_r=0.*

[13] Mark Mazetti and David E. Sanger, "Security Leader Says U.S. Would Retaliate Against Cyberattacks", *New York Times* (March 12, 2013). *http://www.nytimes.com/2013/03/13/us/ intelligence-official-warns-congress-that-cyberattacks-pose-threat-to-us.html?src=twr&_r=0.*

[14] Tom Gjelten, "Is All The Talk About Cyberwarfare Just Hype?" NPR.org (March 13, 2013). *http://www.npr.org/2013/03/15/174352914/is-all-the-talk-about-cyberwarfare-just-hype.*

veat is important, since it is fairly easy to identify potential triggers in this category, such as Taiwan.

The administration's public pronouncements on China have taken on a tougher tone this month, which represents a good step forward—but this is only a first step down a path that, for far too long, we have been traveling too slowly and too weakly. National Security Advisor Thomas Donilon emphasized "the urgency and scope of this problem"—meaning "sophisticated, targeted theft of confidential business information and proprietary technologies through cyber intrusions emanating from China on an unprecedented scale". Donilon then called on China "to investigate and put a stop to these activities" as well as "engage with us in a constructive direct dialogue to establish acceptable norms of behavior in cyberspace".[15] Days later, President Obama himself raised U.S. cyber concerns (of volume, scale, and scope) in a phone call with China's President, Xi Jinping.[16] Sustained U.S. leadership and engagement, at the highest levels, will be required, moving forward.

Since the line between CNE and CNA is thin, with the distinction between the two turning largely on intent, it is crucial that there be consequences for the actor that engages in sophisticated and persistent CNE. The principle applies regardless of the perpetrator. Indeed, one could argue that the only difference between China and Russia in this regard is that China got caught. It is a numbers game, after all. And China may not even be that concerned about getting caught, since the country may have taken a conscious decision to throw as much as possible at us, in terms of human resources dedicated to CNE—in the hope that some, even if not all, of their efforts would yield fruit. Unless and until there are consequences for such behavior, China (and others) have no real reason to care if they are caught in the act of CNE. To date, there have been no significant consequences for China's massive intrusions into critical U.S. networks. By failing to call attention to their CNE campaign (much less retaliating in any way at all) earlier on, we have encouraged it. Last month's White House report announcing a new strategy to mitigate the theft of U.S. trade secrets is at least a step in the right direction.[17]

Russia

Russia's cyber capabilities are, arguably, even more sophisticated than those of China. The Office of the U.S. National Counterintelligence Executive (NCIX) observes: "Moscow's highly capable intelligence services are using HUMINT [human intelligence], cyber, and other operations to collect economic information and technology to support Russia's economic development and security.[18] Russia's extensive attacks on U.S. research and development have resulted in Russia being deemed (along with China), "a national long-term strategic threat to the United States," by the NCIX.

In 2009, the *Wall Street Journal* reported that cyber-spies from Russia and China had penetrated the U.S. electrical grid, leaving behind software programs. The intruders did not cause damage to U.S. infrastructure, but sought to navigate the systems and their controls. Was this reconnaissance or an act of aggression? What purpose could the mapping of critical U.S. infrastructure serve, other than intelligence preparation of the battlefield?

Ambassador David Smith notes: "Russia has integrated cyber operations into its military doctrine; though not fully successful . . . Russia's 2008 combined cyber and kinetic attack on Georgia was the first practical test of this doctrine . . . [and] we must assume that the Russian military has studied the lessons learned".[19] Russia was also behind the 2007 distributed denial-of-service (DDoS) attacks on Estonia (its government, banks, etc.) although Russia denies official involvement. Relying upon "patriotic hackers" guided by government handlers plus a little help from the Russian intelligence service, however, does not alter the reality that activity undertaken by those hackers is state-sponsored and directly implicates Russia.

Hackers and criminals based in Russia have also made their mark. Cyber space has proven to be a gold mine for criminals, who have moved ever more deeply into

---

[15] Donilon, supra.

[16] Steve Holland, "Obama, China's Xi discuss cybersecurity dispute in phone call", Reuters (March 14, 2013). *http://www.reuters.com/article/2013/03/14/us-usa-china-obama-call-idUSBRE92D11G20130314.*

[17] Executive Office of the President of the United States, "Administration Strategy on Mitigating the Theft of U.S. Trade Secrets" (February 2013) *http://www.whitehouse.gov/sites/default/files/omb/IPEC/admin_strategy_on_mitigating_the_theft_of_u.s._trade_secrets.pdf.*

[18] NCIX Report, supra, at p. 5. *http://www.ncix.gov/publications/reports/fecie_all/Foreign_Economic_Collection_2011.pdf.*

[19] "How Russia Harnesses Cyberwarfare", American Foreign Policy Council *Defense Dossier* (August 2012) *http://www.afpc.org/files/august2012.pdf.*

the domain as opportunities to profit there continue to multiply. Russia's slice of the 2011 global cyber crime market has been pegged at $2.3 billion, and there are indications that the forces of Russian organized crime have begun to join up "by sharing data and tools" to increase their take.[20] Just last week, moreover, hackers based in Russia posted what seemed to be personal financial information about the Vice President, the Director of the FBI, and a number of other current and former senior U.S. officials.[21] Russia's history has demonstrated a toxic blend of crime, business, and politics—and there are few, if any, signs that things are changing today. Indeed, as the former ranking member of the KGB in London said recently, Moscow has as many spies in the United Kingdom now as it did in the Cold War.[22] Similarly, former CIA officer Hank Crumpton has said: "I would hazard to guess there are more foreign intelligence officers inside the U.S. working against U.S. interests now than even at the height of the Cold War."[23]

Iran

In April 2012, as mentioned earlier, I testified before a joint hearing of this subcommittee and the Subcommittee on Counterterrorism and Intelligence, on the subject "The Iranian Cyber Threat to the United States."[24] What follows is an attempt to distill the essence of that 9-page statement into just a few paragraphs here.[25]

Iran is investing heavily to deepen and expand its cyber warfare capacity.[26] A range of proxies for indigenous cyber capability also exist. There is an arms bazaar of cyber weapons, and our adversaries need only intent and cash to access it. Capabilities, malware, weapons, etc.—all can be bought or rented. Iran has also long relied on proxies such as Hezbollah—which now has a companion organization called Cyber Hezbollah—to strike at perceived adversaries. Elements of Iran's Revolutionary Guard Corps (IRGC) have also openly sought to pull hackers into the fold. There is evidence that at the heart of IRGC cyber efforts one will find the Iranian political/criminal hacker group Ashiyane;[27] and the Basij, who are paid to do cyber work on behalf of the regime, provide much of the manpower for Iran's cyber operations.[28]

In January 2013, the *Wall Street Journal* reported on "an intensifying Iranian campaign of cyber attacks [thought to have begun months earlier] against American financial institutions" including Bank of America, PNC Financial Services Group, Sun Trust Banks Inc., and BB&T Corp.[29] In the latest chapter in this story, six leading U.S. banks—including J.P. Morgan Chase—were targeted just last week, in "the most disruptive" wave of this campaign, characterized by DDoS attacks.[30] The Izz ad-Din al-Qassam Cyber Fighters claim responsibility for all of these incidents.

There has also been considerable speculation about government of Iran involvement in a number of hacking incidents including against Voice of America, and Dutch firm DigiNotar which issues security certificates. Fallout from the latter case was significant, and affected a range of entities including Western intelligence and

---

[20] Group IB, State and Trends of the Russian Digital Crime Market 2011, p. 6, *http://group-ib.com/images/media/Group-IB_Report_2011_ENG.pdf;* see also *http://group-ib.com/images/media/Group-IB_Cybercrime_Inforgraph_ENG.jpg* (graphics).

[21] Ken Dilanian and Jessica Guynn, "Obama meets with CEOs to push cyber-security legislation", *L.A. Times* (March 13, 2013) *http://www.latimes.com/business/la-fi-obama-hacking-20130314,0,2583428.story.*

[22] Luke Harding, "Gordievsky: Russia has as many spies in Britain now as the USSR ever did", *The Guardian* (March 11, 2013). *http://www.guardian.co.uk/world/2013/mar/11/russian-spies-britain-oleg-gordievsky.*

[23] "More spies in U.S. than ever, says ex-CIA officer." *60 Minutes* (May 10, 2012). *http://www.cbsnews.com/8301-18560_162-57431837/more-spies-in-u.s-than-ever-says-ex-cia-officer/.*

[24] *http://www.gwumc.edu/hspi/policy/Iran%20Cyber%20Testimony%204.26.12%20Frank%20-Cilluffo.pdf.*

[25] For an in-depth treatment of Iran, see Gabi Siboni and Sami Kronenfeld, "Iran and Cyberspace Warfare" in *Military and Strategic Affairs,* Vol. 4, No. 3 (Dec. 2012) at 77–99. *http://www.gwumc.edu/hspi/policy/INSS.pdf.*

[26] Yaakov Katz, "Iran Embarks on $1b. Cyber-Warfare Program," *Jerusalem Post* (December 18, 2011) *http://www.jpost.com/Defense/Article.aspx?id=249864.*

[27] Iftach Ian Amit, "Cyber [Crime/War]," paper presented at DEFCON 18 conference (July 31, 2010).

[28] "The Role of the Basij in Iranian Cyber Operations", Internet Haganah (March 24, 2011) *http://internet-haganah.com/harchives/007223.html.*

[29] Siobhan Gorman and Danny Yadron, "Banks Seek U.S. Help on Iran Cyberattacks", *Wall Street Journal* (January 15, 2013) *http://online.wsj.com/article/SB10001424127887324734904578244302923178548.html.*

[30] Tracy Kitten, "DDoS: 6 Banks Hit on Same Day" (March 14, 2013) *http://www.bankinfosecurity.com/ddos-6-banks-hit-on-same-day-a-5607.*

security services, Yahoo, Facebook, Twitter, and Microsoft.[31] The DigiNotar case, moreover, reflected a new and concerning level of sophistication on the part of Iran and its capabilities. Iran and Hezbollah are also suspected in connection with the August 2012 cyber attacks on the state-owned oil company Saudi Aramco and on Qatari producer RasGas, which resulted in the compromise of approximately 30,000 computers.[32]

On the kinetic side, from Bulgaria to Bangkok, we have seen an uptick in attacks and assassinations (attempted and actual) targeting Israeli, Jewish, U.S., and Western interests. Iranian agents and proxies (Hezbollah) have been implicated, although Iran has tried to distance itself from these incidents and denied responsibility. Also recall the recently thwarted Iranian plot to assassinate Saudi Arabia's Ambassador to the United States on U.S. soil. Based on recent activity, the Los Angeles Police Department has elevated the government of Iran and its proxies to a Tier One threat.

CONCLUSION

Looking ahead, with the described threat spectrum in mind, the United States must strike a careful and powerful balance between offense and defense, to include a well-developed and well-articulated cyber deterrence strategy.[33] Historically, that balance has tilted heavily toward defense.[34] More recently, however, we have seen and heard evidence that the pendulum has shifted significantly. These indicators include General Alexander's testimony before the Senate Armed Services Committee last week (in his capacity as head of U.S. Cyber Command and director of the National Security Agency), in which he referenced and detailed a series of cyber teams attached to Cyber Command—and underscored the role of these teams in contributing to and supporting offensive capabilities.[35] As for U.S. cyber deterrence strategy, it must reflect the best ways and means of raising the (actual and perceived) costs and risks of action, to our adversaries, so as to prevent them from taking steps that would harm U.S. interests.

An "active defense" capability, meaning the ability to immediately attribute and counter attacks, is needed to address future threats in real-time. U.S. companies cannot be expected to go it alone, unassisted, against foreign intelligence services. If a thief robs a bank, the police will not stand idly by as the robber races away with his take. Similarly, the public and private sectors must partner together to prevent major heists on-line—and when private defenses are breached, the U.S. Government must work closely with companies to ensure that there are consequences for the perpetrator(s). Active defense is a complex undertaking however, as it requires meeting the adversary closer to their territory, which in turn demands the merger of our foreign intelligence capabilities with U.S. defensive and offensive cyber capabilities (and potentially may require updating relevant authorities).[36] At the end of the day, however, perhaps the best deterrent—irrespective of the threat/actor—is the ability to recover, reconstitute, and bounce back quickly.

In conclusion, the threat is clear, but it is not monolithic. It will also continue to evolve over time. We may see nation-states intertwine increasingly with proxy ac-

---

[31] Kevin Kwang, "Spy agencies hit by CA hack; Iran suspected," ZDNet Asia (September 5, 2011) *http://www.zdnetasia.com/spy-agencies-hit-by-ca-hack-iran-suspected-62301930.htm.* See also Bill Gertz, "Iranians hack into VOA website," *The Washington Times* (February 21, 2011).

[32] Adam Schreck, "Virus origin in Gulf computer attacks questioned", *Associated Press. http://www.nbcnews.com/technology/technolog/virus-origin-gulf-computer-attacks-questioned-978717.* See also Siboni and Kronenfeld, supra, at pp. 90–91.

[33] Frank J. Cilluffo, Sharon L. Cardash, and George C. Salmoiraghi, "A Blueprint for Cyber Deterrence: Building Stability through Strength", in *Military and Strategic Affairs,* Vol. 4, No. 3 (Dec. 2012) at 3–23. *http://www.gwumc.edu/hspi/policy/INSS.pdf*

[34] Frank Cilluffo and Sharon Cardash, "Defense Cyber Strategy Avoids Tackling the Most Critical Issues" in Nextgov.com (July 28, 2011) *http://www.nextgov.com/cybersecurity/2011/07/commentary-defense-cyber-strategy-avoids-tackling-the-most-critical-issues/49494/.*

[35] Ellen Nakashima, "Pentagon creating teams to launch cyberattacks as threat grows", *Washington Post* (March 12, 2013). *http://www.washingtonpost.com/world/national-security/pentagon-creating-teams-to-launch-cyberattacks-as-threat-grows/2013/03/12/35aa94da-8b3c-11e2-9838-d62f083ba93f_print.html.*

[36] Testimony of Frank J. Cilluffo before the Senate Committee on Homeland Security & Governmental Affairs, "The Future of Homeland Security: Evolving and Emerging Threats" (July 11, 2012). *http://www.gwumc.edu/hspi/policy/Testimony%20-%20SHSGAC%20Hearing%20-%2011%20July%202012.pdf.* See also: Testimony of Frank J. Cilluffo before the House of Representatives' Homeland Security Committee, "The Department of Homeland Security: An Assessment of the Department and a Roadmap for its Future" (September 2012).

21

tors, to include skilled hackers for hire.[37] Now is the time to examine and deconstruct the high-end threat in its many permutations and combinations, so as to devise nuanced and effective counterstrategies and tactics. Thank you again, to the subcommittee and its staff, for the opportunity to testify today. I would be pleased to try to answer any questions that you may have.

Mr. MEEHAN. Mr. Cilluffo, thank you for that very, very sobering assessment.

It is my judgment that we would be better positioned at this point in time to move over as quickly as we can, vote, and then I will ask the members of the panel to, as quickly as possible after the last vote, to return here so we can continue.

Mr. Bejtlich, I would rather you have the comfort of not feeling rushed. Your testimony, the great work that you did with Mandiant, your organization, and your testimony, I think, are too important for us to rush through.

So I thank the panel for your recognition. We look forward to joining you again shortly after votes.

So the committee stands in recess until such time is called back to order. Thank you.

[Recess.]

Mr. MEEHAN. The Committee on Homeland Security Subcommittee on Cybersecurity, Infrastructure Protection, and Security Technologies will now come back into order after our break to conduct our votes.

When we were last together we enjoyed the opportunity to hear Mr. Cilluffo's testimony and we are going to continue now at this point in time to continue to listen to the testimony of our distinguished panel and I am grateful to the panel for your forbearance in working with us during those votes.

So at this time, the Chairman recognizes Mr. Bejtlich for—oh I am sorry—yes, Mr. Bejtlich for your testimony.

Thank you.

STATEMENT OF RICHARD BEJTLICH, CHIEF SECURITY OFFICER AND SECURITY SERVICES ARCHITECT, MANDIANT

Mr. BETJLICH. Thank you Mr. Chairman.

Thank you Ranking Member Clarke and distinguished members of the panel.

My name is Richard Bejtlich and I am the chief security officer of Mandiant.

As chief security officer, part of my role at the company is to protect Mandiant and our customers from digital threats. Last month, Mandiant gave the world a glimpse of one of these threats.

It was a Chinese military unit we identified internally as APT or Advanced Persistence Threat One. We identified that unit as being 61398, which is a term the Chinese military uses itself to assign to this unit.

This unit, we found to be operating approximately 141 companies in the United—primarily in the United States and then in some other locations as well. This is only one of the two dozen or so groups that we track. Many of those are Chinese but there are sev-

---

[37] Frank J. Cilluffo and Joseph R. Clark, "Thinking About Strategic Hybrid Threats: In Theory and in Practice", PRISM 4, no. 1 (December 2012) *http://www.ndu.edu/press/strategic-hybrid-threats.html.*

eral that are Russian and we have a second category of groups that we have not formally attributed, some of which we believe may be from places such as Iran. We are starting to see them for the first time.

As a result of our work, we are encountering these intruders on a daily basis and as we sit here Mandiant is responding to intrusions at dozens of companies, and our software and our services are helping dozens or even hundreds more deal with advance threats.

So you might be wondering why is it that these groups, whether they are from Russia or China or Iran, or other places, why is it that they are able to succeed in compromising targets? I would like to quickly summarize six reasons that we think that is the case.

The first reason is the attacks that were previously reserved for the Government have migrated to the private sector. In other words, what intruders used to use against highly-defended targets are now used against many targets, many of whom are just not positioned to defend themselves.

Second, these attacks are targeting people less than computers or at least conceptually, they are targeting the people. In other words, the intruders are figuring out ways to get you to execute code, visit links, take actions that will result in their computers being compromised. Many times without even the user knowing it.

Third, many of these attacks are coming from the inside and by that I mean it is common now to see attackers go after smaller companies or partner companies or other trusted entities as way to get in to the ultimate target which is another company.

So the larger companies who can afford to defend themselves have become harder and harder topics, so now we are seeing the attacks migrate to the periphery and then they are working their way in.

The fourth reason that these attacks are successful is that there is an imbalance between offense and defense. A single attacker or a group of attackers can keep hundreds or even thousands of defenders busy, there is such an asymmetry there.

As I have noted in the testimony to other committees we do have issues with science, technology, education, and math such that we can have trouble producing the types of engineers, developers, defenders, to protect ourselves.

The fifth reason that many of these attacks are successful is that the countries that harbor these intruders are unwilling to hold them accountable. In many cases, these attacks are government sanctions or directly government targeted and sponsored and this was defiantly the case as we saw of the Chinese military unit I mentioned.

The final reason of these six is that one of the most valuable resources we have in defending ourselves, threat intelligence is unevenly distributed in the Western world honestly.

Not enough defenders have it. The Government has a lot of the information that is required but there are challenges regarding protection of sources and methods, classification, so forth to getting that information at the hands of defenders. Even when that information is available, it is not in a format that you can just put into a tool, put into your processes. There is a lot of reading an e-mail, retyping, and so forth.

So at Mandiant, we try to emphasize machine languages that can exchange information with each other. We have an open standard called OpenIOC that we recommend people take a look at. You put that together and you will have a little better results.

So what to do about it? We do recommend that the Government encourage threat intelligence sharing. We like to stress the threat intelligence does not mean information about individual Americans. It is not personally identifiable information. If you take a look at the report we released, it does not include anyone's name or phone number or credit card or that sort of thing.

Second, we encourage the notification by entities like the Federal Bureau of Investigation to tell companies that they have been compromised. This is a program that has been happening now for several years and it is very effective.

Then finally, we believe that it is important for the Government to hold the most egregious offenders of cyber espionage and other attacks accountable. If it were simply possible to turn down the level of activity slightly to internationally recognized norms or at least historical norms, the private sector in particular would have an easier time defending itself.

Thank you again for the opportunity. I look forward to answering your questions.

[The prepared statement of Mr. Bejtlich follows:]

PREPARED STATEMENT OF RICHARD BEJTLICH

MARCH 20, 2013

Thank you, Chairman Meehan, Ranking Member Clarke, and Members of the subcommittee, for inviting me to discuss threats to our Nation's computer networks. My name is Richard Bejtlich and I am the chief security officer (CSO) at Mandiant. As CSO, part of my role is to understand the threats affecting Mandiant and our customers. I developed these skills as a military intelligence officer with the Air Force Computer Emergency Response Team and as director of the Computer Incident Response Team for General Electric, where I helped defend over 300,000 employees and more than half a million computers.

Mandiant protects the assets of the world's most respected organizations from digital intruders. In addition to responding to high-profile computer security incidents, such as the *New York Times,* we equip security organizations with the tools, intelligence, and expertise required to find and stop attackers who would otherwise roam freely on their networks. We serve more than 30% of the Fortune 100. As I sit here Mandiant is responding to dozens of computer security incidents while our products protect hundreds more organizations from targeted attackers.

We have investigated millions of systems, and we receive calls almost every single day from companies that have suffered a cybersecurity breach. These intrusions affect many industries, including law firms, financial services, manufacturers, retailers, the defense industrial base, telecommunications, space and satellite and imagery, cryptography and communications, government, mining, software, and many others.

It is reasonable to assume that, if an advanced attacker targets a particular company, a breach is inevitable. That surprises many people, but it is the result of the gap between our ability to defend ourselves and our adversaries' ability to circumvent those defenses. There are at least six reasons why attackers continue to successfully exploit this gap in security:

First, the sophisticated, cutting-edge attacks that were previously reserved solely for Government targets have spread to the private sector. Many American corporations, even if they are compliant with appropriate cybersecurity regulations and best practices, are not prepared for these advanced threats.

Second, the attackers are targeting people, not computers. While previous generations of attacks targeted technology and exploited vulnerabilities in software, attackers now target human weaknesses. These attacks focus on individuals and leverage personal information the victim made public via social media. These personalized attacks can be difficult to detect and prevent because they exploit human vulnerabilities and trust.

Third, more attacks are coming from the "inside." It is common to see attackers compromise smaller companies with fewer security resources, and then "upgrade" their access from the trusted, smaller companies to the main target. This problem also occurs when large businesses "acquire" infected networks through a corporate merger or acquisition of a smaller company.

The fourth reason a security gap exists involves an imbalance between offense and defense. A single attacker can generate work for hundreds, if not thousands of defenders. A lone attacker need only breach his target's defenses once to accomplish his goals, but the victim must try to prevent 100% of the attacks. This imbalance is compounded by the critical shortage of skilled security professionals here in the United States.

Fifth, many advanced attackers reside in nations that not only refuse to hold attackers accountable for their actions, but also provide resources and direction to the attackers. So long as state-sponsored criminals can infiltrate American networks and steal American intellectual property without risks or repercussions, these attacks will continue unabated.

Mandiant documented one example of this threat in our APT1 report, released on February 19, 2013. We identified the Chinese cyber espionage unit we call Advanced Persistent Threat 1. We assess APT1 to be Unit 61398, a military hacking unit inside the People's Liberation Army. Unit 61398 is one of approximately 20 groups targeting intellectual property from companies around the world that we assess as operating out of China. Unit 61398 is a single operation that has conducted a cyber espionage campaign against a broad range of victims since at least 2006. From our observations, it is one of the most prolific cyber espionage groups in terms of sheer quantity of information stolen. While it seems clear that Unit 61398 is headquartered in Shanghai, it should be stated that Mandiant tracks dozens of APT groups and not all of them originate in China.

Finally, one of the most valuable resources in detecting and responding to cyber attacks—accurate and timely threat intelligence—is often unavailable to many defenders. Even if defenders have threat intelligence, the means to share it are cumbersome and manual. The United States needs an effective framework for sharing information among commercial entities, and between corporate America and the Government.

Because of these six factors, corporate America continues to be routinely compromised. However, there are steps we can take to significantly narrow the security gap and increase the costs and effort required to steal our intellectual capital.

First, the Government should promote policies that encourage sharing threat intelligence between the private sector and Government, and among private-sector entities. Threat intelligence does not contain personal information of American citizens and privacy can be maintained while learning about threats.

Intelligence should be published in an automated, machine-consumable, standardized manner. Current systems rely on exchanging emails with documents that people must read and transcribe. Mandiant's free OpenIOC standard is one example of a way to codify and exchange threat intelligence.

Second, the Government should support and expand programs whereby law enforcement agencies notify private-sector victims of compromise. Mandiant's recent 2013 M–Trends report shows that only a third of advanced intrusion victims discover breaches on their own. Two-thirds of the time, an external entity, such as the FBI, tells the victim that a foreign entity has stolen their data. External notification is a powerful tool to counter cyber thieves.

Third, the Government should encourage governments hosting or sponsoring the most egregious cyber spies to reduce their activity to internationally acceptable norms. All governments spy to some degree, but they should not target and overwhelm private-sector companies, organizations, and individuals.

Countering digital threats is challenging, but adopting these three recommendations will help reduce the security gap. I look forward to your questions.

Thank you, Mr. Chairman.

Mr. MEEHAN. Thank you, Mr. Bejtlich. Again, I want to express at least in my position as Chairman, the appreciation for what I believe is the courageous move by Mandiant.

I know that there was a great deal of consideration given both with regard to whether you ought to make public what you know and as well as, you know, in effect, sources of methods and other kinds of things that—but at the same time, it created a firm record which I think helped to establish very importantly that activity and I think it was a great effort on behalf of our efforts to secure cyber space.

I now turn to the testimony for Mr. Ilan Berman.

Mr. Berman, the floor is yours.

STATEMENT OF ILAN BERMAN, VICE PRESIDENT, AMERICAN FOREIGN POLICY COUNCIL

Mr. BERMAN. Thank you, Mr. Chairman.

Thank you and thank you, Ranking Member Clarke and the Members of the subcommittee, for the opportunity to appear before you again today.

Let me also take the opportunity to thank you as my colleague did for your leadership on the issues specifically of Iran and cyber warfare. It is a topic that sadly has not yet percolated throughout the width and breath of the U.S. Government, but this committee has really blazed a trail in terms of rising awareness of the issue.

I think it is particularly relevant to the topic today because what you have seen over the last year has been an evolution, a significant evolution, of Iran's capabilities in the exploitation of cyber space, both as a tool of internal repression and as a goal of offensive capability with regard to the asymmetric conflict that is now taking place over the Iranian regime's nuclear program

Let me turn first to the domestic dimensions of what Iran is doing.

A little over 3½ years ago, the fraudulent re-election of Mahmoud Ahmadinejad to the Iranian presidency galvanized the largest organized and sustained protest to the Iranian regime that had occurred since 1979 Islamic Revolution.

That movement, which we have begun to colloquially refer to as "The Green Movement" relied extensively on the internet and on social media such as Facebook and Twitter to organize and to get its message out to the outside world.

As a result, the Iranian regime also relied heavily upon the medium of the World Wide Web to both curtail and then subsequently to repress The Green Movement and opposition elements that have emerged afterwards since that time period.

Today, you are seeing an escalation in terms of what Iran is doing domestically on several different fronts. This is, sort of, a little bit of a greatest hits, if you will. But I think it bears noting that the Iranian regime is building an ambitious project that it calls a "second internet" in which ordinary Iranians who access the internet will be shunted to regime-approved sites. They have also referred to this as the "Halal Internet."

As of October of last year there were about 10,000 computers within the Islamic Republic that were connected to this integrated, they were both private user and public user; governmental user. The ultimate goal of the regime is to force all Iranians to eventually rely on this.

Now, I understand there is a lot of skepticism on that score and it may not be possible to do that, but it bears noting that the Iranian regime has set this as a goal and is perusing that objective.

Iran is also building new on-line and software capabilities to better track and control to social media outlets like Facebook. It has created a domestic homegrown alterative to YouTube, known as Mehr.

It is even beginning the physical persecution and assault on Iran's netizens, on those Iranian citizens that are active in cyber space.

All of this is, I think, driven by something that is approaching that the Iranian regime fears very much, which is the fact that the Iranian regime in a couple of months will face the first presidential election in which Mahmoud Ahmadinejad will not stand for the presidency; he is term-limited.

As a result, this is an election that, no matter how stage-managed the regime will make it, will be a referendum of sorts on the stewardship of the clerical regime, particularly at a time when the western community of nations is bearing down increasingly effectively on Iran with its economic pressure.

It is also augers the potential for a revival of this green wave of opposition elements. As a result, you are seeing Iran invest heavily in domestic repression in anticipation of potential unrest stemming from the elections.

The second, and I think more relevant aspect of Iran's cyber warfare activities here, is what Iran has been doing externally. Iran has evolved a very significant and a maturing offensive cyber warfare capability. Iranian officials now believe cyber war to be, "More dangerous than a physical war," in the words of one Iranian Revolutionary Guard official.

As a result they have invested heavily, particularly at a time when their economy is constrained by Western sanctions in the development of both domestic and international capabilities.

Iran has a, what it calls, a "Cyber Army," which is made up of official, quasi-official, and non-official elements, including hacktivists, and patriotic hackers that pursue objectives that are consonant with regime objectives. They are increasingly carrying out hacking attacks on U.S. financial institutions. In August 2012 they also carried out a hacking attack on Saudi Aramco.

All of this is intended by way of demonstration. What the Iranians are trying to do through these activities is to demonstrate both that they have the capability to reach out and touch the United States and its allies in the event of a conflict, and also that they are willing to do so.

So what all this means is, I think, two major things. First that Iran is a maturing cyber threat. Iran still does not possess the capabilities that are as robust as you see coming out of China, coming out of Russia, but this is not—and I repeat—not an insurmountable problem.

Iran can acquire very quickly and surreptitiously extensive cyber warfare capabilities from the grey and black markets. It can also acquire them from a strategic partner, partners like China and North Korea, where Iran is already collaborating on other strategic spheres such as ballistic missile development and nuclear development.

The second big take-away is that Iran is a qualitatively different cyber actor than the other countries that we have mentioned here today. China and Russia are both focused primarily on cyber theft and cyber espionage. Iran is not. Iran boasts today little by way of a cyber espionage capability.

Rather, what Iran is building is a cyber capability that is retaliatory in nature, and it is built largely around Iranian perceptions of the unfolding conflict that is now on-going between itself and the West over its acquisition of a nuclear capability.

This makes the situation with Iran's cyber warfare capabilities particularly vulnerable—volatile because while these other countries are pursuing a degree of diplomatic normalcy with the United States, Iran is not. Iran is actually anticipating in erecting its cyber infrastructure a catastrophic breakdown of diplomatic relations with the West in which cyber will play a role in conjunction with kinetic effects in war fighting against the West.

I will stop there.

Thank you.

[The prepared statement of Mr. Berman follows:]

PREPARED STATEMENT OF ILAN BERMAN

MARCH 20, 2013

THE IRANIAN CYBER THREAT, REVISITED

Chairman Meehan, distinguished Members of the subcommittee: Thank you for the invitation to appear before you again today. Let me begin by commending the House Homeland Security Committee for its continued leadership on the issue of Iran and cyber warfare. It is a topic that is of the utmost importance to the safety and security of the United States.

A year ago, I had the privilege of testifying before this committee regarding the Islamic Republic's cyber warfare capabilities, and the threat that they could potentially pose to the American homeland. Today, the questions that were posed at that time are more relevant than ever.

The past year has seen the Iranian regime evolve significantly in its exploitation of cyber space as a tool of internal repression, with significant consequences for country's overall political direction. During the same period, Iran also has demonstrated a growing ability to hold Western targets at risk in cyber space, amplifying a new dimension in the asymmetric conflict that is now taking place over the Iranian regime's nuclear program.

IRAN VERSUS THE WORLD WIDE WEB

A little over 3½ years ago, the fraudulent reelection of Mahmoud Ahmadinejad to the Iranian presidency galvanized the largest outpouring of opposition to the Iranian government since the 1979 Islamic Revolution. That protest wave, colloquially known as the Green Movement, made extensive use of the internet and social media in its anti-regime activities. Iranian authorities responded with a similar focus—one that has both persisted and expanded in the wake of their successful suppression of the Green Movement during the 2009/2010 time frame.

Most conspicuously, the Iranian government is moving ahead with the construction of a new national internet system. As of October 2012, some 10,000 computers—from both private users and government offices—were found to be connected to this "halal" or "second" internet, which is aimed at isolating the Iranian population from the World Wide Web.[1] The eventual goal of the Iranian regime is to force all Iranian citizens to use this system. Iranian officials thus have announced plans to reduce internet speeds within the Islamic Republic, as well as increase costs of subscriptions to Internet Service Providers (ISPs) within the country.[2]

Along the same lines, Iran in December 2012 launched Mehr, a home-grown alternative to YouTube that features government-approved video content designed spe-

[1] Sara Reardon, "First Evidence for Iran's Parallel Halal Internet," *New Scientist* no. 2886, October 10, 2012, *http://www.newscientist.com/article/mg21628865.700-first-evidence-for-irans-parallel-halal-internet.html.*

[2] Reporters Without Borders, "The Enemies of Internet: Iran," March 12, 2013, *http://surveillance.rsf.org/en/iran/.*

cifically for domestic audiences.[3] Iranian authorities also reportedly are working on new software suites designed to better control social-networking sites (a hub of activity during the 2009 protests and after).[4]

The Iranian regime likewise has expanded control of domestic phone, mobile, and internet communications. In the months after the summer 2009 protests, Iranian authorities installed a sophisticated Chinese-origin surveillance system to track and monitor phone, mobile, and internet communications.[5] They have since supplemented such tracking with methods intended to limit access to such media. Just this month, for example, Iranian authorities blocked most of the virtual private networks (VPNs) used by Iranians to circumvent the government's internet filters.[6]

The Iranian regime has stepped up its detention and intimidation of reporters and activists who utilize the world wide web as well. Its tool of choice to do so has been the Cyber Police, a dedicated division of the country's national police that was established in January 2011.[7] Earlier this year, the European Union added the Cyber Police to its sanctions list for the unit's role in the November 2012 torture and death of blogger Sattar Beheshti while in police custody.[8] In all, some 58 journalists and "netizens" are currently imprisoned by Iranian authorities, according to the journalism watchdog group Reporters Without Borders.[9]

The Iranian regime also has established a new government agency to monitor cyber space. The Supreme Council on Cyberspace was formally inaugurated by Iranian Supreme Leader Ali Khamenei in April 2012, and serves as a coordinating body for the Islamic Republic's domestic and international cyber policies.[10]

All of these activities have been propelled by a sense of urgency on the part of the Iranian leadership. This June, Iranians will go to the polls to elect a new president. That political contest, although sure to be stage-managed by clerical authorities, will nonetheless serve to some degree as a referendum on the Iranian regime's stewardship of the nation amid deepening Western sanctions. It could also see renewed activity by Iran's opposition forces, which have been politically sidelined in recent years. Iran consequently has made what the U.S. intelligence community terms "cyber influence" a major governmental focus, clamping down on internet activity "that might contribute to political instability and regime change."[11]

FROM DEFENSE TO OFFENSE

Iran's offensive cyber capabilities likewise continue to evolve and mature. Over the past 3 years, repeated cyber attacks have targeted the Iranian nuclear program, with considerable effect. In response, Iranian officials have focused on cyber space as a primary flashpoint in their regime's unfolding confrontation with the West. Officials in Tehran now believe cyber war to be "more dangerous than a physical war," in the words of one top leader of Iran's Revolutionary Guard Corps (IRGC).[12]

As a result, the Iranian regime has made major investments in its offensive cyber capabilities. Since late 2011, the Iranian regime reportedly has invested more than $1 billion in the development of national cyber capabilities.[13] As a result, Iranian

[3] David Murphy, "Iran Launches 'Mehr,' Its Own YouTube-Like Video Hub," *PCMag,* December 9, 2012, *http://www.pcmag.com/article2/0,2817,2413014,00.asp.*

[4] Golnaz Esfandiari, "Iran Developing 'Smart Control' Software for Social-Networking Sites," *Radio Free Europe/Radio Liberty,* January 5, 2013, *http://www.rferl.org/content/iran-developing-smart-control-software-for-social-networking-sites/24816054.html.*

[5] Steve Stecklow, "Special Report: Chinese Firm Helps Iran Spy on Citizens," *Reuters,* March 22, 2012, *http://www.reuters.com/article/2012/03/22/us-iran-telecoms-idUSBRE82-L0B820120322.*

[6] "Iran Blocks Use of Tool to Get around Internet Filter," *Reuters,* March 10, 2013, *http://www.reuters.com/article/2013/03/10/us-iran-internet-idUSBRE9290CV20130310.*

[7] University of Pennsylvania, Annenberg School of Communications, Iran Media Program, "Internet Censorship in Iran," n.d., *http://iranmediaresearch.org/sites/default/files/research/pdf/1363180689/1385/internet_censorship_in_iran.pdf.*

[8] "EU Sanctions Iran Judges, Cyber Police for Rights Abuse," *Agence France-Presse,* March 12, 2013, *http://www.france24.com/en/20130312-eu-sanctions-iran-judges-cyber-police-rights-abuse.*

[9] Reporters Without Borders, "Intelligence Ministry Admits Arresting News Providers, Blames Foreign Media," February 20, 2013, *http://en.rsf.org/iran-intelligence-ministry-admits-20-02-2013,44099.html.*

[10] University of Pennsylvania Iran Media Program, "Internet Censorship in Iran."

[11] James R. Clapper, "Worldwide Threat Assessment of the US Intelligence Community," Statement for the Record before the Senate Select Committee on Intelligence, March 12, 2013, 2, *http://www.dni.gov/files/documents/Intelligence%20Reports/2013%20ATA%20SFR%20for%-20SSCI%2012%20Mar%202013.pdf.*

[12] "Iran Sees Cyber Attacks as Greater Threat than Actual War," *Reuters,* September 25, 2012, *http://www.reuters.com/article/2012/09/25/net-us-iran-military-idUSBRE88O0MY20120925.*

[13] Yaakov Katz, "Iran Embarks on $1b. Cyber-Warfare Program," *Jerusalem Post,* December 18, 2011, *http://www.jpost.com/Defense/Article.aspx?id=249864.*

officials now claim to possess the "fourth largest" cyber force in the world—a broad network of quasi-official elements, as well as regime-aligned "hacktivists," who engage in cyber activities broadly consistent with the Islamic Republic's interests and views.[14] The activities of this "cyber army" are believed to be overseen by the Intelligence Unit of the IRGC.[15]

Increasingly, the Iranian regime has put those capabilities to use against Western and Western-aligned targets. Between September 2012 and January 2013, a group of hackers known as the Izz ad-Din al-Qassam Cyber Fighters carried out multiple distributed denial-of-service (DDoS) attacks against a number of U.S. financial institutions, including the Bank of America, JPMorgan Chase, and Citigroup. Due to the sophistication of the attacks, U.S. officials have linked them to the Iranian government.[16]

A similar attack attributed to the Iranian regime took place in August 2012, when three-quarters of the computers of Saudi Arabia's Aramco state oil corporation were targeted by a virus called "Shamoon." The malicious software triggered a program that replaced Aramco's corporate data with a picture of a burning American flag at a predetermined time.[17]

The Iranian regime has also begun to proliferate its cyber capabilities to its strategic partners. Iran reportedly has provided the regime of Syrian dictator Bashar al-Assad, now locked in a protracted civil war against his own people, with crucial equipment and technical assistance for carrying out internet surveillance.[18] This, in turn, has helped the Assad regime to more effectively target and neutralize elements of the Syrian opposition.

A MATURING THREAT

Despite recent advances, Iran's cyber capabilities are still nascent when compared to those of China and Russia. There is broad agreement among technical experts that the cyber threat posed by the Iranian regime is more modest than that posed by either Moscow or Beijing, at least for the moment. Yet Iran's activities in, and exploitation of, cyber space should be of utmost concern to American policymakers, for several reasons.

The first is opportunity. The capabilities "gap" that currently exists in Iran's ability to carry out sustained and significant cyber attacks against U.S. infrastructure could close rapidly. This is because all of the resources that the Islamic Republic requires, whether human or technological, can be acquired quickly and comparatively cheaply from gray and black market sources. Additionally, recent years have seen the Iranian regime receive significant inputs to its strategic programs from abroad, most prominently from China and North Korea. This assistance is known to have furthered Iran's nuclear and ballistic missile capabilities, perhaps significantly so. Given this history, there is every reason to conclude that cooperation between Iran and its strategic partners is on-going in the cyber domain as well.

The second is intent. Over the past 2 years, no fewer than five distinct cyber assaults have targeted the Iranian regime's nuclear effort. (At least one, moreover, has been determined to be domestic in origin, suggesting the Iranian regime faces an internal cyber threat as well). As a result, Iranian officials have come to believe—with considerable justification—that conflict with the West has already begun. The cyber attacks that Iran has carried out in recent months provide a strong indicator that the Iranian regime is both willing and able to retaliate in kind.

Finally, it is worth noting that Iran represents a qualitatively different cyber actor from either Russia or China. While both the PRC and the Russian Federation actively engage in cyber espionage against the United States, each has repeatedly avoided mounting a cyber attack so disruptive that it precipitates a breakdown of diplomatic relations with Washington. Iran, by contrast, could well countenance exactly such a course of action in the not-too-distant future.

In his most recent testimony to the Senate Select Committee on Intelligence, Director of National Intelligence James Clapper noted that "Iran prefers to avoid di-

---

[14] "Iran Enjoys 4th Biggest Cyber Army in World," FARS (Tehran), February 2, 2013, *http://abna.ir/data.asp?lang=3&Id=387239.*

[15] University of Pennsylvania Iran Media Program, "Internet Censorship in Iran."

[16] Nicole Perlroth and Quentin Hardy, "Bank Hacking was the Work of Iranians, Officials Say," *New York Times,* January 8, 2013, *http://www.nytimes.com/2013/01/09/technology/online-banking-attacks-were-work-of-iran-us-officials-say.html?pagewanted=1&_r=0.*

[17] Nicole Perlroth, "In Cyberattack on Saudi Firm, U.S. Sees Iran Firing back," *New York Times,* October 23, 2012, *http://www.nytimes.com/2012/10/24/business/global/cyberattack on saudi-oil-firm-disquiets-us.html?pagewanted=all.*

[18] Ellen Nakashima, "Iran aids Syria in Tracking Opposition via Electronic Surveillance, U.S. Officials Say," *Washington Post,* October 9, 2012, *http://articles.washingtonpost.com/2012-10-09/world/35500619_1_surveillance-software-syrians-president-bashar.*

rect confrontation with the United States because regime preservation is its top priority."[19] This, however, has the potential to change rapidly in the event of a further deterioration of the current, tense standoff between the international community and Iran over its nuclear program. Iranian officials have made clear that they see cyber space as a distinct warfighting medium in their unfolding confrontation with the West.

Government officials increasingly recognize this fact. A draft National Intelligence Estimate now circulating within the U.S. Government reportedly identifies Iran as one country which would benefit substantially from having the capability to target and disable sectors of the U.S. economy.[20] What is not yet visible, however, is a comprehensive approach to understand, address and mitigate Iran's ability to hold American interests and infrastructure at risk via cyber space.

CYBER SPACE AND THE IRANIAN BOMB

Back in October, then-Secretary of Defense Leon Panetta warned publicly that the United States could soon face a mass disruption event of catastrophic proportions, a "cyber Pearl Harbor" of sorts. "An aggressor nation or extremist group could use these kinds of cyber tools to gain control of critical switches," cautioned the Defense secretary. "They could derail passenger trains, or even more dangerous, derail trains loaded with lethal chemicals. They could contaminate the water supply in major cities, or shut down the power grid across large parts of the country."[21]

Such a scenario is plausible, although the U.S. intelligence community currently judges its likelihood to be "remote," at least in the near term.[22] However, geopolitical events could dramatically alter this assessment, and incentivize threat actors in cyber space to target both American interests and infrastructure.

In this regard, no scenario is more urgent or potentially dangerous than the unfolding crisis over Iran's nuclear program. Despite a massive expansion of Western economic pressure over the past year, the Iranian regime still shows no signs of slowing its drive toward atomic capability. To the contrary, Iranian officials have taken a defiant stance, laying out the need for an "economy of resistance" with which they will be able to weather economic pressure from the United States and Europe until such time as they cross the nuclear Rubicon.[23] As such, the near future could see a further escalation of the crisis, perhaps including the use of force against Iran by one or more nations.

Should that happen, cyber war with Iran could become a distinct possibility. So, too, could Iranian targeting of American forces, interests, and infrastructure, with potentially devastating effects on the security of the U.S. homeland.

Mr. MEEHAN. Well on that note Mr. Berman—and I am sure we will follow up on that testimony.

Now the panel will hear from our last distinguished panelist; Mr. Libicki the floor is yours.

STATEMENT OF MARTIN C. LIBICKI, SENIOR MANAGEMENT SCIENTIST, RAND CORPORATION

Mr. LIBICKI. Thank you and good afternoon Chairman Meehan, Ranking Member Clarke, and other distinguished Members of the subcommittee. Thank you for the opportunity to testify today on cyber threats and protecting American critical infrastructure.

On September 11, 2001, 3,000 people died, and the physical damage was upwards of $200 billion. On September 12, the country responded. The next dozen years saw 6,000 dead, tens of thousands injured, and costs well over a trillion dollars.

---

[19] Clapper, Statement for the Record, 5.

[20] Nicole Perlroth, David E. Sanger and Michael S. Schmidt, "As Hacking against U.S. Rises, Experts Try to Pin Down Motive," *New York Times*, March 4, 2013, *http://mobile.nytimes.com/2013/03/04/us/us-weighs-risks-and-motives-of-hacking-by-china-or-iran.xml;jsessionid=8304-B2493AF15262FDA4F217DDF0CAFE?f=19.*

[21] Elisabeth Bumiller and Thom Shanker, "Panetta Warns of Dire Threat of Cyberattack on U.S.," *New York Times*, October 11, 2012, *http://www.nytimes.com/2012/10/12/world/panetta-warns-of-dire-threat-of-cyberattack.html?pagewanted=all&_r=0.*

[22] Clapper, Statement for the Record, 5.

[23] "Iran Leader Calls for 'Economy of Resistance,'" *Agence France-Presse*, August 23, 2012, *http://news.yahoo.com/iran-leader-calls-economy-resistance-134523014.html.*

If cyber is similar, one might conclude that even though an attack on the United States may be damaging, the cycle of response and counter-response may be far more consequential.

The issue of how the United States should manage crisis and escalation in cyber space is addressed in the recently-published Rand Report of that name. I now want to take the opportunity to summarize seven salient points in that document.

The first point is to understand that the answer to the question you all have been here asked, is this cyber attack an act of war, is not a conclusion, it is a decision.

Cyber wars are wars of choice. A country struck from cyber space has the opportunity to ask, what would be the most cost-effective way to minimize future suffering, and depending on the circumstances it might be war, alternatively it might not be.

Second, is to take the time to think things through. Computers may work in nano-seconds, but the target of any response is not the computer, in large part because even if a computer is taken out a substitute may be close at hand. The true target of a response are those who command the cyber warriors, that is people. But people do not work in nano seconds. Persuasion and dissuasion of people work at roughly the same speed whether or not these people command cyber war or any other form of war.

Third is to understand what is at stake, which is to say, what the United States hopes to gain by making the attackers cease their efforts. This goes for both responding to cyber attack and to responding to what might be deemed intolerable levels of cyber espionage.

The fourth is to not take possession of a crisis unnecessarily, or at least if you are going to do so, do so on your own terms, which is to say, don't back yourself into a corner where you always have to respond whether doing so is wise or not.

Fifth is in responding craft and narrative that helps take the crisis where you want to take it. In some cases in fact, the narrative might have to allow the attacker to cease its attacks without losing face by doing so.

Sixth is to figure out what norms of conduct in cyber space, if any, work best for the United States. It may be encouraging that last week both the United States and China agreed to carry out high-level talks on cyber norms, but there are a lot of questions to work through.

As an example, where does one draw the many lines among cyber war, cyber sabotage, cyber crime, cyber espionage, and violations of international trade law?

The seventh is to manage cyber escalation wisely. That means remembering that the other side will probably react to what you yourself do, yet in cyber space, using tit-for-tat measures to modulate the other side's escalation can be a very uncertain and crude tool.

Of course, one of the best ways of avoiding a 9/12 in cyber space is to avoid a 9/11 if you can. In that regard, I would like to toss out a few ideas. These are born of the notion that while there are many sources of cyber insecurity we wouldn't be worried about a catastrophic cyber attack or much of the advanced persistent system threat for that matter were it not for malware. Malware itself does not happen without systematic weaknesses in software architectures and implementations.

In a world that spends $60 billion a year on security for instance, a much, much smaller total of that is spent eradicating vulnerabilities in widely-used software programs. Allocating Federal money from buildings to finding and thereby reducing the vulnerabilities in these programs, may be money well spent.

The same logic, unfortunately, does not hold for machine control software such as SCADA Systems. Such software was designed for a relatively benign environment, not the internet. Vulnerabilities in such software are so common that they will take a long time to fix completely.

In the mean time, leaving such systems connected to the rest of the internet may not necessarily be a particularly good idea. Isolation will reduce the odds of a catastrophic attack more than probably anything else will.

Finally we need to rethink information sharing. There is nothing wrong say with two chemical companies sharing information with one another on cyber attacks, but we really need to hear not from the companies themselves but from the security firms that work for them, because they are the folks who actually understand what happens to the companies when they get attacked.

The folks that they need to hear from are again not so much the companies themselves, although that is a good thing, but those who build software for such companies.

Well, thank you very much. I am happy to answer any questions you might have.

[The prepared statement of Mr. Libicki follows:]

PREPARED STATEMENT OF MARTIN C. LIBICKI [1]

MARCH 20, 2013

MANAGING SEPTEMBER 12 IN CYBERSPACE [2]

On September 11, 2001, terrorists attacked the United States. Three thousand people died and the physical damage was upwards of two hundred billion dollars. On September 12, the country responded. The United States strengthened its homeland security. We went to war twice. Over the next dozen years, the United States lost six thousand in combat. Ten to twenty thousand were seriously injured. Total additional expenditures exceeded a trillion dollars. I point this out not to criticize the policies that followed—but to indicate that even though an attack on the United States may be damaging, the cycle of response and counter-response may be far more consequential.

Accordingly, even though a cyber-9/11 may be costly, it would be shortsighted to evaluate the threat in terms of immediate damage without considering how the United States would manage such a crisis in order to yield an outcome that works best for the American people. That is, we are right to be worried about a "9/11 in cyber space," but we also ought to worry about what a "9/12 in cyber space" would look like. Indeed, one of the best reasons for working hard to avoid a 9/11 in cyber space is avoid having to deal with a 9/12 in cyber space. That noted, because a cyber

[1] The opinions and conclusions expressed in this testimony are the author's alone and should not be interpreted as representing those of RAND or any of the sponsors of its research. This product is part of the RAND Corporation testimony series. RAND testimonies record testimony presented by RAND associates to Federal, State, or local legislative committees; Government-appointed commissions and panels; and private review and oversight bodies. The RAND Corporation is a nonprofit research organization providing objective analysis and effective solutions that address the challenges facing the public and private sectors around the world. RAND's publications do not necessarily reflect the opinions of its research clients and sponsors.
[2] This testimony is available for free download at *http://www.rand.org/pubs/testimonies/CT383.html*.

9/11 (or what looks like a 9/11) might happen, it is worthwhile to think about what we do the day after.

The issue of how the United States should manage crisis and escalation in cyber space is addressed in the recently-published RAND document of that name.[3] I now want to take the opportunity to touch on some of the salient points in that document, as well as follow-on thoughts.

The first point is to understand that the answer to the question—is this cyber attack an act of war?—is not a conclusion, but a decision. In physical combat, such a question may be meaningful: If your neighbor's tanks are in your backyard heading for the capital, then war is on. But such a question is usually the wrong one to ask about cyber war. True, cyber war can disrupt life even on a mass scale. Cyber warfare can enhance conventional military power. But, it cannot be used to occupy another nation's capital. It cannot force regime change. No one has yet died from it. And, Stuxnet notwithstanding, breaking things with ones and zeroes requires very particular circumstances. A cyber attack, in and of itself, does not demand an immediate response to safeguard National security. Instead, a country struck from cyber space has the opportunity to ask: What would be its most cost-effective way to minimize such future suffering? If war fits the bill (and other nations understand as much), the victim of a cyber attack could declare that it was an act of war and then go forth and fight. Perhaps making war can persuade the attacker to stop. Yet, war also risks further disruption, great cost, as well as possible destruction and death—especially if matters escalate beyond cyber space. Or a country may look at policies that reduce the pain without so much risk—such as by fixing or forgoing software or network connections whose vulnerabilities permitted cyber attacks in the first place.

Second is to take the time to think things through. Computers may work in nanoseconds, but the target of any response is not the computer—in large part because even if a computer is taken out a substitute can be close at hand. The true target of a response is those who command cyber warriors—that is, people. But, people do not work in nanoseconds. Persuasion and dissuasion of people work at roughly the same speed whether or not these people command cyber war or any other form of war. A corollary error is to assume that a confrontation in cyber space is inherently unstable—thereby necessitating being a quicker draw than the other guy. It is precisely, because unlike with nuclear war, a nation's cyber war capabilities cannot be disarmed by a first strike, there's not the same need to get the jump on the other guy, just as there is not the same need to match his offense with your offense, when it's your defense that dictates how much damage you are likely to receive.

Third is to understand what is at stake—which is to say, what you hope to gain by making the attackers cease their efforts. This goes for both responding to cyber attack and responding to what might be deemed intolerable levels of cyber espionage. With cyber attack, what you are trying to prevent is not the initial attack, but the next attack—the effects of which might be larger than the initial attack but may also be smaller. (This is particularly true if the initial attack teaches the immediate victims, that, say, making industrial controls accessible to the internet may not have been the smartest idea.) As for espionage, we really have no handle on how to evaluate the damage that takes place to the country when other countries see what we don't want them to see.

Fourth is not to take possession of the crisis unnecessarily—or at least do so only on your own terms. That is, do not back yourself into a corner where you always have to respond, whether doing so is wise or not. It is common these days, to emphasize the cost and consequences of a cyber attack as a National calamity; last week the Director of National Intelligence proclaimed it as the primary short-term threat to the Nation. Making such arguments tends to compel the United States to respond vigorously should any such cyber attack occur, or even merely when the possible precursors to a potential cyber attack have been identified. Having created a demand among the public to do something, the government is then committed to doing something even when doing little or nothing is called for. In some cases, it may be wiser to point out that the victim had a feckless cyber security posture. In other cases, downplaying the damage may be called for. The more emphasis on the pain from a cyber attack, the greater the temptation to others to induce such pain—either to put fear into this country or goad it into a reaction that rebounds to their benefit. Conversely, fostering the impression that a great country can bear the pain of cyber attacks, keep calm, and carry on reduces such temptation. Correspondingly, despite good arguments in favor of drawing red lines for deterrence purposes—"if you do this, I will surely do that"—the cost of being credible is that if deterrence

---

[3] Martin Libicki, *Crisis and Escalation in Cyberspace,* Santa Monica CA (RAND), MG–1215–AF.

fails, such a declaration tends to constrain one into carrying out retaliation. To do nothing or nothing much, at that point, tends to hollow all deterrent postures, and not just in cyber space. Given the inevitable ambiguities associated with the consequences and causes associated with cyber attacks, inflexibility may also demand a response well before the facts are clear. There are careful trade-offs that have to be made.

Fifth is to craft a narrative that facilitates taking the crisis where you want to take it. Narratives are, essentially, political morality plays, in which the United States has to select a role that puts it in a good light while retaining basic consistency between the facts of the matter, as well as with its previous narratives. Part of crafting a narrative requires finding the right role: Does the United States want to portray itself as a victim of cyber attack? As the righteous enforcer of international norms? As the superpower that demands respect? Narratives also have to find a role for the attacker, and the definition of such a role may, in some cases, have to encourage and accommodate the attacker's graceful and face-saving retreat from belligerence. After all, the odds that an attack in cyber space arises from, miscalculation, inadvertence, espionage with unintended consequences, or the actions of a rogue actor are nontrivial.

Sixth is to figure out what norms of conduct in cyber space, if any, work best for the United States. Last week both the United States and China agreed to carry out high-level talks on cyber norms. Although nearly 4 years of Track II negotiations with the Chinese (in which I participated) have yielded meager results, there are still some grounds for optimism. But, first we have to address some salient questions. To what extent can the Laws of Armed Conflict apply in a domain where the patterns of collateral damage are poorly understood, where the distinction between civil and military is difficult to discern, where it's getting harder and harder to know where your information sits, and where the transparency required for neutrality simply does not exist? Where does one draw the many lines among cyber war, cyber crime, cyber espionage, and violations of international trade rule? Is it in the U.S. interest to make unconstrained espionage a casus belli? How well should states be able to monitor (let alone enforce) compliance before it can assure itself that the norms are worth having?

Seventh is to manage cyber escalation wisely. This not only means remembering that the other side will react to what you do, but also understanding what a crude tool counter-escalation may be for influencing the other side. Consider that with Stuxnet, it took many tries to get the desired effect. The Iranians may not have known they were under attack until they read about it in the *New York Times*. It is also unclear whether we would have had much damage assessment had the centrifuge plant not been under independent inspection. To further illustrate what the fog of cyber war may mean to escalation control, assume a defender wants to place in an opponent's mind the thought that if he escalates and the defender will counter-escalate proportionally. But in cyber space what the attacker does, what he thinks he did, and what the defender thinks he did may all be different. The defender can only react to what he thinks the attacker did. That is because the defender's systems are usually different than the attacker's. Equivalence between perception of the attack and the intended response may be inexact. Then there's the similar difference between the defender's response and the attacker's perception of what was done in return. After all this, the attacker may think the retaliation was proportional, understated, or went overboard in crossing counter-escalation red lines—red lines that were not originally crossed by himself. The effect is akin to playing tennis on a rock-strewn court.

In sum, while I believe it is certainly worthwhile effort to prevent a future 9/11 in cyber space—and understanding the nature of the threat is an important component of that effort—similar levels of care and thought needs to be given to how to manage a potential 9/12 in cyber space. If not, we may find, as with the historical 9/11, that the consequences of the reaction and counter-reaction are more serious than the consequences of the original action itself.

Mr. MEEHAN. Well, thank you, Mr. Libicki.

Thank you for, all of the panel, for your opening statements. You have touched on collectively a number of critical areas for us in terms of framing the nature of the threat and commentary and more specific fashions as to where we see this thing going.

I am grateful today to have the presence of the Chairman of the full Committee on Homeland Security and without objection I will go out of order and allow the Chairman to make some opening comments or if he has a few observations or questions for the panel, I would allow that to be entertained as well.

Mr. McCAUL. Well, I thank the Chairman for your generosity, and thank you to the witnesses for being here today.

This is an issue of growing concern by the day. Today we just saw North Korea attack South Korea in a denial-of-service attack in an attempt to shut down its government. We have the representative from Mandiant here who reported recently that the Chinese military has hacked into our Federal Government to steal our military secrets. I think for me most disturbingly is what has happened not just with China, Russia, but as you Mitch and Mr. Berman, with Iran.

I think the fear has always been that you know Russia is good at espionage and crime, so is China; they steal things, but it is the countries that disrupt and bring things down that is probably the thing that keeps us up at night the most.

So I want to ask this question because the Iranian attack was particularly interesting in the sense that the attack against Aramco in the Persian Gulf was a very destructive attack that knocked out 20,000, 30,000 hard drives bringing them down in energy sector. The attack against our financial institutions in the United States on the other hand was a very disruptive denial-of-service attack crashing servers but not destroying. But the point remains that Iran has this capability to destroy.

I asked the question, why the difference in attacks, and the answer was, well they are red-lining us. They are testing us. They want to know how far they can go with this before we actually ultimately respond.

So my question, I guess I will start with Mr. Berman, anybody else on the panel is: At what point do we respond? At what point do these attacks—and we have debated what constitutes an act of warfare, but at what point do these attacks truly constitute an act of warfare to be met with an in-kind response?

Mr. BERMAN. Well, thank you, sir, and I appreciate you asking such an easy question to get this ball rolling.

This is actually, I think, the $64,000 question. It is not a question that can be answered by myself or by anybody here on this panel. It is a decision made by the National Command Authority with regard to framing a deterrence posture in cyber space and then also carrying out retaliatory attacks if it chooses to do so; if it perceives that a red line has been crossed.

I would point out that you outlined very nicely sort of the Iranian motivation and the Iranian way of thinking about what it is doing; these cyber attacks that it has carried out against U.S. financial institutions. By the way, not only U.S. financial institutions, before it attacked Bank of America and JPMorgan Chase, it took aim at Israel's central bank, at Bank Hapoalim.

So these are all demonstration attacks to a greater or lesser extent, to demonstrate that it has the ability to reach out and touch the United States and its coalition partners if the conflict over its nuclear program goes south in some substantial way.

Iran is also doing something, which I think is more tangible and is of greater concern, which is the outlining how it would act definitively in the event of a breakdown in relations and coalition warfare against Iran over its nuclear program. The attack on Saudi Aramco can be seen as a signaling mechanism by which Iran is telegraphing to the international community that it plans to target C4I capabilities in the event of overt warfare with regard to Iran.

This is—I think it is important to note that the Iranians are thinking about cyber warfare operationally in that context. Whether or not we choose to respond to these attacks is an entirely different question and it is one that stems from how we define the threat, and whether or not we actually do, as Mr. Libicki said, do draw definitive red lines that forces us to retaliate.

Mr. CILLUFFO. Mr. Chairman, to build on that point, and I agree very much with what Ilan has just expressed. But, I mean, one way to think about some of these cyber threats, especially—and I am reminded of how we used to discuss state-sponsored terrorism in the 1980s and 1990s. You have state-sponsored, state-sanctioned, and state-directed. What makes cyber so complex is the plausible deniability factor, obviously.

Just like Iran has turned to its proxies to engage in kinetic attacks, obviously they will also look to proxies if they build-out the capacity to do so in the cyber domain. One thing that is worth noting, though, is whether it is IRGC or whether it is Quds Force, they are also home to one of the most sophisticated hacker underground communities that has been around for quite some time, noted as Ashiana. Some of these capabilities where they may provide what we would call in the military "commanders intent," they are not necessarily even sure who is calling the shots where and when.

There might be a good news story on the U.S. side. Maybe it was more difficult to get to some of our energy companies the way they were able to do so vis-á-vis Saudi Aramco. That said, if the balloon goes up, I am more concerned that they turn to their proxies in a kinetic kind of way where cyber becomes—it enhances the lethality. It is a force-multiplier effect.

That is why I put it in the chart, why I put it at the blinking high-red in my prepared remarks. That is something that we shouldn't discount. U.S. interests overseas have long been lightning rods for terrorist activity. I think you would see a lot of similar sort of activity in the region. So, they are very good at electronic warfare. They have been doing this for a long time. So, here cyber is just another instrumentality to achieve those sorts of objectives and something we need to take seriously.

Mr. MCCAUL. Let me just say thank you to the panel.

I also want to again thank the Chairman and Ranking Member for your generosity in letting me sit here and ask questions. Also, the work you have done on this issue—I appreciate it and I look forward to the point where we end up marking up legislation on this committee.

Thank you.

Mr. MEEHAN. Thank you, Mr. Chairman. We are grateful for your support for the important work of this committee and look forward to working with you. As you can see, the testimony from this distinguished panel I think is helping to put in context the importance of what we are doing. That is a big part of what we are trying to approach today.

Because I—Mr. Cilluffo, I thank you, as I recognize myself for 5 minutes of questioning. For your setting the table in the sense of us trying to put our arms around this, it is easy to get lost not only in the broad scope of the threat, but the failure to distinguish among different parts of the threat.

You were articulate in explaining that there are various levels that actually get us to the places where we may be able to do a lot. Mr. Bejtlich and others discussed cyber high—we can do the deal with big parts of it that we probably are principally interested in this issue of state-sponsored activity.

That even within the realm of state-sponsored activity, the question becomes: What becomes the kind of motivating factor that is tied with the capability that then becomes the creator of an intentional act?

Now, we have seen actions as recently as this week that have been tied back, at least according to published reports, to Iran—once again, more sophisticated attacks against our banking system. I would be interested in your interpretation of those attacks, what you think they are, and how realistic they may be as whether they are precursors to something which is simply probing, or part of a pattern of activity that may indicate future vulnerability for the United States.

Mr. CILLUFFO. Mr. Chairman, thank you for that question. I think you do ask one of the most difficult questions. Because what I tried to do is parse out the computer network exploit from computer network attack. The one issue that is sort of in between both is the cyber equivalent of intelligence preparation on the battlefield.

So, the fact is, is our critical infrastructure, the domain of this subcommittee and the committee generally speaking, are all identifiable and they have been probed and they have been mapped. At the end of the day, they have not necessarily been, at least with the actors we are most concerned about, looked at from a computer network attack perspective, but the fact that they have probed these systems, what other motive could they possibly have? They are not stealing secrets here. It is not espionage. It is to be able to come up with a potential battle plan in the future.

Big concern. When you see the Iran clickety-clack of the keyboard behind that, then we have got some real significant lines, maybe not in the sand, but in the silicon that have clearly been crossed. Again, I think that Iran is going to look at it through a kinetic lens most directly.

In terms of these DDOS attacks, the distributive denial-of-service attacks, they are becoming more powerful. You can rent a botnet for very little that can cause major disruption. That is not the same as destruction, but it can get to the point where companies that live and breathe on just-in-time inventories, that live and breathe on the ability to connect with their customers immediately, it has a huge impact.

I just came back from Estonia, where I brought a bunch of my students that are part of an executive MBA program there, and they don't have bank tellers anymore. It is all computerized.

Mr. MEEHAN. So, this capacity, as we have identified it, we focused on Iran most recently, but we have also spoken about North

Korea and the capacity to be able to go out into the marketplace and therefore even enhance their capability by participating with other kinds of nation-state actors or others who have the ability to generate this.

Mr. Berman, you used a——

Mr. CILLUFFO. I am actually more concerned about North Korea in some ways.

Mr. MEEHAN. North Korea.

Mr. CILLUFFO. It is about survival of the regime, wild cards, and traditionally crime tries to penetrate the state. In North Korea, it is the inverse. The state is penetrating organized crime and they are engaged in all——

Mr. MEEHAN. Mr. Berman, you spoke a great deal about that. You used the word "retaliatory" as being a precursor to some activities, and we see what happened this week in South Korea. So, explain to me how you interpret those in the context of whether they are retaliatory actions, and then most—the greatest concern is the added word "volatility."

Do they in combination create what you—this panel had testified before when we were asking questions about the willingness of the Quds Force to carry out an act of terrorism on United States soil. Then months later, we saw it. So, I respect your vision. What do you see happening now?

Mr. BERMAN. Well, thank you, sir. I appreciate the kind words.

I agree with my colleague. I think what we are looking at here is a mismatch between capability and intent. The Iranians are not nearly as sophisticated and persistent as the Chinese and even the Russians. But what you have is a set of actors—and I say "set" because what we are talking about here is not just Iran, but also North Korea—that is hyper-politicized in the sense that both are engaging in active diplomatic warfare with the international community over their respective nuclear programs, over sanctions, over some deviant behavior, that may force them—or may cause them to lash out in ways that we would not predict.

One of the saving graces of our China cyber problem and our Russia cyber problem is that while we may not be comfortable with the scope, we in general understand the direction. That is missing in our calculation with regard to Iran and increasingly with regard to North Korea. The shared geopolitical driver here is that both regimes are under growing international stress as a result of their rogue behavior. But it is also the type of international stress—economic, diplomatic, financial—that is forcing them to lash out in unpredictable ways.

As a result, as Frank said, the cyber component of this behavior becomes very, very germane because if Iran seeks to retaliate and it is a perceived retaliation, because Iran already, if you look at the way it has written in speeches, the way it has spoken—its officials have spoken, they see themselves already at war with the West on some level. They see cyber as an adjunct to all the other things that they are doing in order to respond.

Mr. MEEHAN. I look forward to following up, but at this point my time has expired. So I turn it to the Ranking Member, Ms. Clarke, for her questions.

Ms. CLARKE. Thank you very much, Mr. Chairman.

I would like to start with Dr. Libicki. I am a bit concerned about how we classify the activities that are taking place. You know, this is a homeland security committee, and I want to just ask you, I understand that a lot of your work deals with questions of state-on-state cyber conflict and international issues. That is the domain of foreign-oriented departments, such as State and Defense. But I also appreciate your testimony on needing to be careful in our messaging of the cyber threat, and not calling everything cyber war.

I, for one, believe that the vast majority of malicious cyber activity is directed against consumers in the private sector, and it is not appropriate for the military to play a role—the lead role in protecting against this type of activity. The threats are, indeed, great, but that doesn't mean it requires a military response.

Do you agree, or do you have any thoughts on the right way to talk about cyber threats without doing it in a way that over-militarizes our response?

Mr. LIBICKI. Well, if you going to respond with the military, I suppose your most important question is: Is it to your advantage to get into a war? If the answer is no, then you may think of other ways of responding.

In many ways, however—and I mentioned—you mention narrative, if the United States goes around saying how vulnerable it is to cyber attack and how much it is afraid of cyber attack, then it sets up a situation in the minds of others that the United States is particularly sensitive if it gets attacked through this method.

If we, however, adopt a posture, insofar as we can, that in fact these things happen to computers all the time, that computers can be occasionally volatile, but things happen to them, and that we are really talking about levels of annoyance, to a certain extent you can remove some of the disincentive for others to attack the United States, because the impact on what we do will not be very great.

Ms. CLARKE. So, let me dig a little bit deeper, because what we are trying to get a sense of is, you know, we have a domestic responsibility to private citizens whose identity may be stolen, the sort of garden-variety types of malicious cyber activity.

We are trying to make a distinction here, because this whole hearing we have been talking about really an international connection. For the average American, it is like, you know, I just don't want my medical information sold in Russia, or, you know, I don't want my identity to be—how do we make that distinction and then how do we sort of create a flexible infrastructure that enables us to be sensitive enough to know where certain forces enter versus others?

Mr. LIBICKI. Well, pretty much everything we are talking about, at least at the U.S. level, is considered a crime. Sometimes we can get our hands on these folks, sometimes we can't. Some of my colleagues pointed out because we don't have the cooperation of the Government.

To a large extent, therefore, that means in these areas defense becomes a lot more important than it would other places. I think there is a great deal that the United States can do, that the United States Government can do to beef up defenses. I think there is a lot of good work being done by DHS. I think there are ways they can carry out more activities.

I had mentioned reducing the vulnerabilities in a lot of software. I think a certain amount of progress is being made, but by no means fast enough. I think we can encourage a great deal of resilience. Standards of resilience may, at least, give you some guidelines as to what constitutes resilience in the first place.

We have by no means exhausted the list of things we can do at the domestic level to reduce the level of threat to where, in fact, at a foreign policy level we can start ignoring it.

Ms. CLARKE. Let me ask Mr. Bejtlich, it seems that most consumers and corporations still look to anti-virus software as state-of-the-art. Recently, however, it seems that the market has been clamoring for new approaches, particularly focusing on resilience and mitigation strategies when companies are inevitably hacked.

Over the years, have you noticed a real shift in companies' level of awareness of the cybersecurity threats to their business, and have companies been realizing that traditional anti-virus approaches just won't cut it and are they now looking for more sophisticated approaches to mitigating their risk?

Mr. BETJLICH. The best-performing companies that Mandiant interacts with have generally gone through a traumatic experience, where they have had a large intrusion, and they have realized that all of the approaches that they have adopted were not sufficient to stop the intruder, and they tend to adopt more of a fast-and-accurate detection model, followed by response and containment.

You still need anti-virus. You still need these other technologies that will deal with a certain group of threats, but you have to realize there will be that gap a sophisticated or determined intruder will get through, and then you need to find them quickly and deal with them.

So, while I will say that is becoming more accepted at the top tier, at the small- or medium-business level, they don't have the resources, the awareness. It is truly a big problem at those other levels.

Mr. MEEHAN. Thank you, Ranking Member Clarke.

The Chairman will now recognize Mr. Perry for his questions, if he has them.

Mr. PERRY. Thank you, Mr. Chairman.

Thank you, gentlemen. It is a fascinating topic, and I am hopeful it is one that we can find some bipartisan cooperation on, although I think it is vexing every single one of us in the room how we work on that.

With that, I would like to just get right to a whole host of questions.

Regarding supply-chain cyber-threats, is that something that is legitimate? Should we be concerned? What countries would export such things so that users or purchasers would know, look, there is a potential danger in buying from X company, if that is appropriate to ask that kind of question.

Anybody?

Mr. CILLUFFO. First crack at this. I think your colleagues at the House Permanent Select Committee on Intelligence, Mr. Rogers and Mr. Ruppersberger, did a fantastic service in identifying some of the potential concerns vis-á-vis Huawei and ZTE in particular.

But I think it raises a bigger set of questions. We need to start baking security requirements into the design of our systems. Start with our weapons platforms and systems, and then we have got to start looking at critical infrastructure. To me, that is partially a Federal acquisition reform issue.

We actually need to prioritize contracting acquisition opportunities for those that are baking security requirements. Yes, that is a big concern. I don't care how much security you have up here, if it is built on quicksand, who cares?

Mr. PERRY. So, with that, I mean, and with the Ranking Member's questions, I wonder, how much—first of all, is this information available to normal purchasers and users? Are products to thwart the threats that we are discussing commercially available on a wide scale right now?

Mr. BETJLICH. There is an emerging industry of companies, like Mandiant, who recognize that threats will get through, and you have to find them quickly and deal with it.

However, there is still a large industry built around the legacy systems. To piggyback on Frank's comments, we have seen, through our own intrusion response, as the primary target gets harder, you move farther out into the ecosystem, and eventually you will get to the point where the ecosystem is hard enough that you have to start with the hardware, and then you work your way back in.

So maybe that is why very hard targets, like the military, they have come to realize this is the No. 1 problem they have. It is not the No. 1 problem in private sector, but as the private sector gets its act together, you are gonna see the threat migrate to those supply chain problems.

Mr. PERRY. As a—I have spent over 30 years in the military, so I am really familiar with the IPB process and some other things that were discussed here, and I think that is kind of where most of us head.

But I think in terms of selling this, for lack of a better phrase, to the public about the need for this and then how we address it, I think we are gonna have to discuss what is in it for them, and I think that it is hard to get your brain wrapped around that.

So with that, let's say I have a firm that, like just about any other district, that makes some very critical components, whether it is defense or manufacturing, that they compete globally, who do they report it to? Like, what is the first phone call they make if they suspect? Where do people go?

Mr. BETJLICH. I would encourage anyone who believes that you are on the shopping list for an advanced threat, such as China or Russia, to have a relationship with your local FBI office.

They will tell you whether or not the technology you produce or the business you are in is of interest to a foreign power. They will help you from that point forward.

However, cyber still remains the one area where if there is a dead body on the ground, there is no police you call who will run to you and do the forensics and all that. For the most part, it is still a private-sector response.

That is changing a little bit. I mean, in critical infrastructure, you can call the ICS–CERT and they will send a team. There is more of that going on.

But my company was created 9 years ago because there was no one to call. So we are the ones that go out, and we answer the call on these intrusions.

Mr. CILLUFFO. Mr. Perry, could I——

Mr. PERRY. Absolutely. Please do.

Mr. CILLUFFO [continuing]. Very briefly. This is a little philosophical way to think about it. At the end of the day, we need to get to the 80 percent solution, which is not going to stop the APT threats. It is not gonna stop Russia. It is not going to stop China.

Russia, by the way, is more in the HUMINT business, and they have integrated cyber to be part of the human intelligence business. That is why I would say from a tradecraft standpoint, they are actually higher than China, even.

But the one thing I would suggest is you get to that 80 percent solution so you can free up the limited resources that Uncle Sam has to focus on the real bad actors. Right now, they can't delineate between the kid in his mother's basement or the foreign intelligence service threat.

We have got to get to the point where we can free up resources, limited as they are, to focus them on the higher end. That—you can't expect a company to defend themselves against the SVR. It is just—they are in the business of business.

So we have got to build the business case. Any legislation should be comprehensive, but it should also incorporate incentives. It should also incorporate liability exemption. We do need to have—we don't want this to be a cigarette wrapped in asbestos, forgive the pun, but we really do need to build up our security capabilities, focus the limited resources on the high-end threat spectrum, and the private sector can handle the rest.

But right now, there is an unfair playing field. They are defending against Chinese intelligence services. That is just not fair.

Mr. PERRY. Thank you.

Mr. MEEHAN. Thank you, Mr. Perry.

Now, we have not only been called to vote, but the time has expired on our vote. But we are trying to—Mr. Vela has participated with us, and I am very grateful for his presence.

Mr. Vela, do you have a question for the panel that you would like to——

Mr. VELA. Yes. I will make them quick.

My question is: Given the significant energy production that we have in States like Texas, Pennsylvania, and the Dakotas, what is the real-life cyber threat to the energy sector in those places?

Mr. BETJLICH. So, Mandiant has responded to intrusions affecting the energy sector. We have not seen the intruders getting into the industrial control systems, but they have been in the corporate networks, and they have taken design documents, plans, other intellectual property.

This has also been well-documented in the open press, in places like the *Christian Science Monitor* and elsewhere. So there is a real threat from espionage into the energy sector in the United States.

Mr. VELA. So it is not just a matter of threat to the energy trading. It goes more to the intellectual property and the things that those companies work with.

Mr. BETJLICH. Yes, sir.

Mr. MEEHAN. Let me thank this very, very distinguished panel.

Once again, we have been called to votes, and I think rather than inconvenience you a second time, we are delighted and thankful that you have taken the time.

I point all of those who are interested in this issue not just to the testimony you have given and the written testimony, but to the voluminous work each of you has done and the way you have helped us to frame this issue. I am hopeful that we can continue to work with you in this year ahead as we not only frame the issue, but work towards legislation to help us address the issues.

I would like to ask unanimous consent that a statement from Mr. Dean Picciotti, president of Lexington Technology, a Philadelphia-based cybersecurity consulting firm, be included in the record.

Without objection, so ordered.

[The information follows:]

STATEMENT OF DEAN PICCIOTTI, PRESIDENT, LEXINGTON TECHNOLOGY AUDITING

MARCH 20, 2013

Lexington Technology appreciates the opportunity to submit testimony for this important subcommittee hearing on protecting the Nation's critical infrastructure.

It is important to explain the risks we face and how new legislation can strengthen our ability to protect this critical element of our country's civilian infrastructure. We need uniform minimum standards for cybersecurity defense and disaster recovery.

ABOUT LEXINGTON TECHNOLOGY

Founded in 2011 by long-time industry leaders, Lexington is a Philadelphia-based cybersecurity consulting firm that provides advice and services to mass transit systems, State court systems, school districts, and other government and quasi-government agencies. The firm's efforts are focused mainly on the systems relied upon for our region's data security. We spend most of our workdays in the cybersecurity "trenches." It is from this view point that we offer this testimony.

WHAT'S AT STAKE?

The Earth is, crisscrossed by networks of wires, cables, waves, pulses, and signals. The computer systems that operate this world are all around us, yet just under the surface. Driven to design simplicity and ease of use into most systems, developers have learned to cleverly disguise the fact that you are even using a computer. But computers are, in every imaginable size, supporting every conceivable application—and it is all connected.

- Smartphones, laptops, mobiles, desktops
- ATMs, store barcode scanners, credit card swipe machines
- Telephone systems, television systems
- High-rise elevator and HVAC system controls
- Ordering systems, payment systems, money-moving systems
- Factory production systems, assembly lines
- Food processing and packaging systems
- City water systems, sewage systems, rail lines, traffic signals
- Electric and gas utility processing/production and distribution

As the world becomes increasingly interconnected and reliant on computers to run everything from our coffeemakers, rail roads, elevators, court systems, and nuclear plants, cyber space has become the fifth domain of warfare, after land, sea, air, and space.

It is important to keep in mind however, that the threats are not only from foreign shores but also from within our borders. Destabilizing a nation's cyber-infrastructure is not an exact science. The results are not necessarily foreseeable or controllable. However, forcing a nation-state into chaos without an identifiable adversary is a perfect tool for the asymmetric attacks of terrorists. There is little lead time. There is little chatter. Assembling the devices necessary rarely requires embargoed or highly-regulated materials.

A FLAWED CONVERGENCE STRATEGY AND AGING INFRASTRUCTURE

Two decades ago, in an attempt to save money in the growing software-based process control and automation industry, companies began to explore the logistics, implications, and benefits of converging the pathways that control desktops, servers, and industrial equipment. Many malicious attacks take advantage of the inherent flaws in this convergence strategy.

One of the flaws in convergence is the introduction of USB Memory Sticks (the same ones you may have on your keychain) to the factory floor. Industrial equipment rarely has USB ports, but because of convergence these devices, which now share networks with office-grade equipment, are integrated (knowingly or unknowingly) with desktop computers. As a result of this convergence, power plants, pipeline networks, refineries, mass transit, high-rise HVAC, elevator systems, water and sewage plants, grain elevators, communications networks and other large-scale System Control and Data Acquisition (SCADA) applications are susceptible not only to internet-delivered attacks but also to USB stick-borne viruses, even when the network is completely isolated from the internet.

Imagine these systems infiltrated by malware, crashing, rendered useless, at least temporarily. The data grid fails. The power grid fails. The communication grid fails. The transportation grid fails. Imagine the potential for panic—financial and otherwise—in the face of these cascading network failures.

Our infrastructure presents a dangerous combination of known and unknown vulnerabilities in the cyber domain, strong and rapidly expanding adversary capabilities, and limited threat and vulnerability awareness. While we are more network-dependent than ever before, improved interconnectivity has drastically increased the threat of unauthorized entities from taking control of, or damaging our infrastructure. No longer is the threat limited to physical attacks or embedded personnel. Successful and attempted attacks may be initiated with complete anonymity from anywhere in the world.

Our daily life, economic vitality, and National security rely upon our information technology infrastructure. As our complex economy demands more and more connectivity each year, we are simultaneously increasing the potential attack surface. The operation of our economy depends on a vast array of interconnected communications and power sources that, at present, stand vulnerable to attack.

RECENT ATTACKS

In January 2008 a 14-year-old boy derailed 4 trains in Poland using a modified television remote control.

During the summer of 2011 several law enforcement agencies had their private emails leaked by Lulzsec, a small group of hackers that exploited weak SQL and PHP implementations on websites. This allowed them to deface websites and obtain username and password lists of authorized users. With that information, Lulzsec exploited the fact that many users use the same username and password combination on multiple sites: Disrupting our economy and reducing productivity.

In 2012 a 24-year-old man gave a presentation at the DEF CON conference entitled "How to Hack All the Transport Networks of a Country". His presentation showed how a test to see whether free rides could be obtained allowed him to attach to internal processes, gain client data including financial information, and then how he was able to gain access to the System Control and Data Acquisition systems operating the entire transit system. He believes that the same, or similar, vulnerabilities exist in every transit system network in the world.

Cyber incidents have increased dramatically since 2010 reports of nation-state, individual, and group attacks on infrastructure are occurring with regular frequency. In 2011, the DHS U.S. Computer Emergency Readiness Team (US–CERT) received more than 100,000 incident reports, and released more than 5,000 actionable cybersecurity alerts and information products. Preliminary reports have that number increasing dramatically in 2012 and beyond.

The aftermath of Hurricane Sandy presented us with a brief glimpse of the dangers and hardship of a major transit system being shut down by a known natural occurrence. Imagine the devastation both in human lives, economic loss, and confidence should a coordinated attack bring down multiple transit systems or cause transit vehicles to be used as weapons of destruction.

Recognizing the serious nature of this challenge, President Obama has made cybersecurity an administration priority and he reaffirmed the importance of securing our critical information systems by signing the Executive Order on Improving Critical Infrastructure Cybersecurity and Presidential Policy Directive (PPD) on Critical Infrastructure Security and Resilience on February 12, 2013.

We need a concerted effort and substantial funding on the part of our Federal Government to create uniform minimum standards to protect, secure, and constantly monitor critical information and control systems. We also need uniform minimum standards for disaster recovery in the event of a successful attack. Organization and continued funding of these efforts has to be a top priority if we are to keep these systems operating safely.

MINIMUM STANDARDS

In order for the organizations that operate our critical infrastructure to be able to protect cyber systems from attack we need legislation that standardizes the minimum expectations for reasonable cybersecurity defenses and disaster recovery preparation.

We need to make sure our critical infrastructure operators understand the expectations and have the information, tools, knowledge, and rights to continually update and harden systems against an ever-evolving threat. We cannot depend solely on Government agencies to be able to detect attacks and then drop in and take over unfamiliar systems with the speed and knowledge necessary to circumvent or recover from an attack. That can only be accomplished by the individuals that work with those disparate and complex systems every day.

The United States Government should work with non-Federal critical infrastructure organizations to provide the necessary resources to meet the highest standards and best practices available today and as set by the National Institute of Standards and Technology and the Pentagon as they're published and modified in the future.

In conclusion, our critical infrastructure, our economy, and even our lives depend upon secure information technology systems and industrial control systems. The number and frequency of attacks are increasing and significant changes are needed now to protect our transportation systems to prevent a future disaster that could cripple our economy and/or result in large numbers of casualties.

Mr. MEEHAN. I want to thank the witnesses for their valuable testimony and Members for their questions. The Members of the committee may have additional questions for the witnesses, and I will ask you to respond to those in writing if they are submitted with 10 days. We will hold the record open.

Without objection, the subcommittee stands adjourned. Thank you.

[Whereupon, at 4:01 p.m., the subcommittee was adjourned.]

○

www.ingramcontent.com/pod-product-compliance
Lightning Source LLC
Chambersburg PA
CBHW080342290526

45791CB00009BA/2696